CHAIM SOUTINE
1893-1943

MAURICE TUCHMAN

LOS ANGELES COUNTY MUSEUM OF ART

*This is the first comprehensive exhibition of paintings by Chaim Soutine
in the United States since the Museum of Modern Art's presentation,
directed by Monroe Wheeler, in 1950. It is the largest ever held in this
country. I have made the present selection of ninety paintings
from almost 600 works known to me in the course of several years of
intensive research on Soutine's oeuvre. The objective has been to
present a fresh view of Soutine by choosing paintings which have rarely
been seen, except for those great and renowned works which can not
be experienced too often. Emphasis has been placed on Soutine's
production of the twenties, for reasons of quality, and in particular on
the Céret paintings (1919-1922), of which nineteen are now shown.
In the thirties and until the artist's death in 1943, Soutine's production
and esthetic achievement declined, and only nineteen works from this
fourteen-year period are here presented. A complete view of the late
Soutine is still not possible, for many of these works have been
and continue to be kept from the public eye by a few Parisian
collectors of Soutine.*

*For assistance in preparing the essay, I want to thank Mrs. Jane
Livingston who made careful, intelligent and helpful comments about it.
Mrs. Livingston also worked closely with me on the Bibliography,
as well as at every stage in the preparation of the entire book-catalog,
and the lengthy organization of the exhibition itself. To her I owe
a special debt of gratitude.*

*I also want to thank Mr. Sidney Brody, Mr. and Mrs. Klaus Perls,
Mr. Andras Kalman, Mr. and Mrs. Theo Brennahum, Mrs. Irene Shapira
and Monsieur Jean-Francois Bonpaix for special assistance, as well
as Henry Hopkins, James Monte and Miss Frieda Kay Fall, who read
the manuscript.*

I am also grateful to Mr. Jack Tworkov for his Afterword *on Soutine.*

Maurice Tuchman

Chaim Soutine was born in Smilovitchi, a Lithuanian village of about 400 inhabitants near Minsk, in 1893. He was the tenth of eleven children of a pitifully poor Jewish mender, not, as has been said, a tailor. This distinction was important in the *shtetl* — the small East European Jewish community — where the social hierachy was extremely subtle. In Zborowski and Herzog's informative monograph on shtetl culture, a lady from the old world is quoted as saying, "the ones who make the soles on the shoes are considered low *prost* [roughly translated, uncouth, unmannered people]. Those who make the upper parts of the shoes are already higher."[1] Soutine's family was on the bottom rung of the social ladder. Sholom Aleichem said of the characters in his writings about shtetl life that they were "experts" on hunger: Soutine was such an expert.

Soutine rarely reminisced about his boyhood but he did speak of it, with bitterness, to a few friends late in his life. From their accounts, particularly from the report of the painter Michel Kikoine, a friend from Smilovitchi, one can glean the tenor and chronology of his boyhood. Smilovitchi was a gray mass of ramshackle wooden houses. The sky above was almost eternally a somber gray-green. One of Soutine's earliest recollections was of his fascination with the play of sunlight and shadow in the house. Through a window of the family dwelling, Soutine's father could be seen from the street, "squatting in a Buddha-like position, working at his mending at all hours of the day." His mother was "old before her time...always worried and uncommunicative...not particularly affectionate with her numerous progeny."[2] At the age of thirteen Soutine already loved to draw, and would sketch on any scrap of paper he could find, or on the walls with charcoal. He was ridiculed for this by his family (his father wanted him to become a cobbler or a tailor), and was actually punished physically for his "crime." Two of his older brothers constantly taunted him, saying, "A Jew must not paint," and they beat him mercilessly. Their cruelty became almost a ritual. Soutine would flee his brothers and hide himself in the woods near the village until hunger forced him home. He would return to find milk and warm black bread, which he dearly loved, laid on the table. But when he crept into the kitchen he would be beaten again by his waiting brothers.[3] Soutine also recalled being beaten for stealing a kitchen knife to trade for drawing crayons. One day, when Soutine was about sixteen, he approached a pious Jew and asked him to pose for a portrait. The next day this man's son and his friends thrashed Soutine and left him for dead. He was eventually rescued, but it was a week before he could walk again. A complaint was lodged

Soutine, *Self-Portrait*, c. 1920, oil on canvas. Whereabouts unknown

against the aggressors by Soutine's mother, and the boy was granted an amendment of 25 rubles.

With the money, Soutine and Kikoine set off for Minsk to become artists. Kikoine relates that "our first instructor in Minsk was a man named Krueger, who gave private lessons and guaranteed success in three months."[4] A year later, Soutine went to Vilna and applied at the Ecole des Beaux Arts for a three year course. In an unpublished biography of Soutine, Henri Serouya says that Soutine "was asked to draw a cone, a cube and a pitcher. Being terribly nervous, he made a mistake in perspective which caused him to be refused admission. He wept at the feet of Professor Rebakoff. Moved by his tears, the old director took pity on Soutine and gave him another opportunity to pass the examination, this time alone in the classroom. He accomplished the exercise perfectly and became a brilliant student at the school."[5] He was taught a kind of heavily modeled realism, dense and laborious, and for the first time saw reproductions of works by old masters. In his private sketches, which were always done from nature, he chose subjects evocative of sadness, misery and suffering. His friends recall, for example, that he staged a Jewish burial. He had Kikoine lie down and cover himself with a white drape, then encircled the shrouded figure with candles and drew the scene.[6] He hid everything he made, and even at this early period he viciously destroyed anything which did not please him.

Soutine was twenty years old before he fully left behind him the culture of the shtetl. It is doubtful that the effects of his youth and early training as an artist actually were — or could have been — really abandoned in any significant sense. But even in the most informative commentaries on Soutine there is practically no reference to the recurring echoes of shtetl life in his painting. Thus Soutine's art, though certainly recognized for its greatness, has for decades been at least partially misunderstood as eccentric.

In the shtetl, extremely high value was placed on emotional expressiveness and feeling. Students and former inhabitants of the shtetl constantly point to the texture of daily life as being full of energy and noise and agitation. Expressions of vitality in almost any form were regarded as healthy and desirable. "Life in the shtetl is lived with abounding zest," commented Zborowski and Herzog.[7] These writers describe the concept of "sholem bayis," or household peace, as "a state of dynamic equilibrium" rather than "unruffled serenity." In their words, "A happy household is a swirl of people, all busy, all talking. There may be arguments

Photograph of Soutine. Courtesy La Bibliothèque des Arts, Paris

9

and nagging, mutual recriminations. All this is part of being expressive, part of showing one's affection and interest, part of sharing in the experiences of one's family . . . The equilibrium is possible because affection and anger are not in the least incompatible."[8] Soutine's characteristically vigorous animation of the canvas surface is a reflection of the intense emotionalism of the shtetl. "The vocabulary of the East European Jew's heart," wrote the renowned scholar Abraham Heschel, "has only one sound: 'Oy!'"[9] This cry, a mixture of joy and sadness and enthusiasm, exudes from all of Soutine's paintings. The flow of passion in them sometimes seems to overwhelm the forms, calling to mind an analogy to that Yiddish literature (Ashkenazic) in which all form and structure is submerged in an outpouring of sentiment, a passion both intellectual and ecstatic.[10] Soutine's painting is also reminiscent of the writing of such authors as Sholom Aleichem, who in Alfred Kazin's words, "present certain particularities, traits, sensations, habits or witticisms, even certain *biological characteristics, as a physical substance."*[11]

The Jew's high regard for feeling is characteristically expressed in words. "The paramount role of words," say Zborowski and Herzog, "is suggested by the popular notion that every human being has assigned to him at birth a definite quota of them. When his quota of words is expended, he will die . . . In this highly verbalized culture, words are more than a medium of communication. The word is a force in itself, a tool. More than that, the word itself embodies substance — the Hebrew root is the same for 'word' and for 'thing' or 'object'. Thus the word endows its referent with existence."[12] Howe states that one "spoke not of a beautiful thing but of a beautiful deed or event."[13] Traditionally, the importance of verbal communication has implied suspicion and disparagement of visual expression. Drawing and painting were considered sinful. "Thou shalt not make unto thee any graven image, or any likeness of anything that is in heaven above, or that is in the earth beneath, or that is in the water under the earth," reads the Second Commandment. Solomon condemned painting, "the sight whereof entices fools to lust after it, and so they desire the form of a dead image, that hath no breath . . . they that make them, they that desire them, and they that worship them, are lovers of evil things. . . ."[14] Distruct and even fear of the visual was manifest on other levels and in different areas of shtetl life. The process of *looking,* for example, was said to be dangerous. A pregnant woman was taught to fear "mislooking herself," that is, she was to avoid looking at anything that might harm the unborn child. "A pregnant woman must be on the alert every minute of every day . . . if a mother 'mislooks herself on an animal' she may give birth to a monster and it will be said that she bore a calf or a dog. An ugly or misshapen person is commonly referred to as a 'mislooked one.'"[15] After the baby was born it was thought that it might be harmed by being *looked at* too much. The child was protected from the gaze of outsiders. The mother or nurse would distract a spectator's attention by diverting his glance to something else. An "evil eye" was blamed for any common ailment at any age, and the exclamation, "No evil eye!," was always used as a precaution. (A powerful antidote to visually caused problems was speech. There was a professional "talker-away" — *opshprekher* — of badness.)[16] The act of looking and seeing was associated with terrible power — hence the phenomenon of the orthodox Jew who would avoid the sight of women, and would adopt an habitually furtive glance.

In the shtetl the Christian image of a Divinity was regarded as inferior because it was corporeal, represented visually on an icon. The shtetl child had "no vivid image of Him"; God was "conceived of as a disembodied and all-prevasive presence,"[17] a concept consistent with the prohibition against graven images.

Soutine is singular among twentieth century artists in his willful insistence on the surpassing importance of the concretely perceived thing. Precisely because the visual experience was so impugned in his youth, Soutine placed supreme value upon the particularity of the object. He focused obstinately on the shibboleths pertaining to sight; violating these shibboleths became the basis of his art, and accounts in part for its intense seriousness and air of utter necessity.

There are several well-known stories of Soutine's search for the right model. When he left Paris to wander over France it was always in search of the "right" landscape. If he was inspired by a potential model he would go to any lengths to force the person to pose for him. He would resort to pleas, threats, insults or even bribery to get the person stationed before him. Legends quickly arose about his obstinate refusal to yield up a chosen subject. When he installed a huge beef carcass in his studio, pouring buckets of blood on it continually to keep its red flesh color, he painted it until its putrid stench brought the police and health authorities. Even then he persuaded them to let him keep it a while longer. "Art is more important than sanitation!" he insisted.[18] When a satisfactory subject was finally obtained he would paint it again and again.

It is clear that the shtetl's injunction against "seeing" produced in

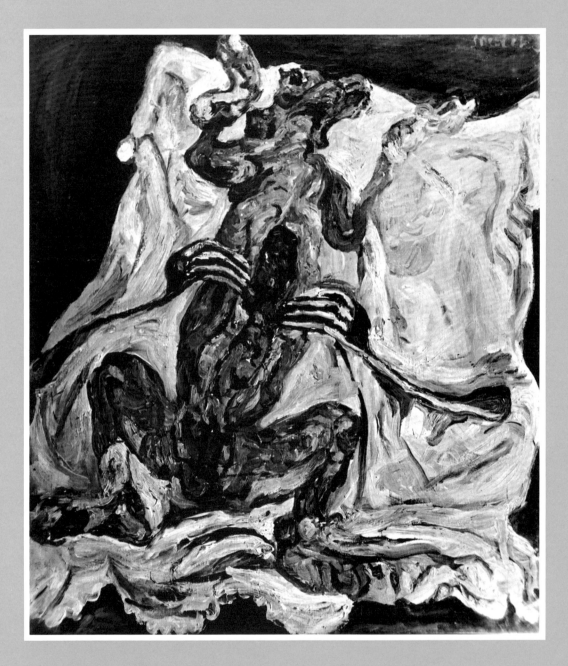

Soutine the most compelling need to experience visual sensation. It can also be demonstrated how specific subjects and themes reflect his shtetl conditioning. Soutine chose subjects which were particularly proscribed by the shtetl too often to be coincidental. Sometimes — in spite of his attempt to forget the shtetl, and in spite of his manifest dislike for nostalgic or folkloric subjects — a distinct, if semi-conscious, childhood theme appears in his work. The most direct examples of this are Soutine's famous images of hanging, splayed fowl. The motif is singular in Soutine's oeuvre for in some cases it clearly is *not* a literally perceived subject, nor could it have been; the fowl appears to be in motion. Soutine's art generally imbues the static with an inner turbulence: *Fowl* is possessed of actual *Pl. 71* movement. Given Soutine's obsessive need to have the subject there before him, one can only account for these pictures by reference to a shtetl custom with which Soutine would have been familiar. On the morning of the Eve of Yom Kippur — the Jewish Day of Atonement — there occurred in the shtetl a ritual of absolution. In the words of Zborowski and Herzog, the shtetl "would be busy with the beating of the scapegoat. Actually the beating of the goat might more accurately be called *the whirling of the fowl.* In the ancient days . . . the scapegoat was sent out into the desert, carrying the sins of the community. The shtetl rationale has transformed the quadruped into a fowl, and instead of being sent away to the desert, it is consumed by the family at the [post-] Yom Kippur feasts. . . . The fowl . . . is whirled about the head of the penitent, with an appropriate prayer."[19] It is tempting to speculate that just as Soutine's "whirling fowl" is a psychological scapegoat, so too are the uniformed domestics and servants Soutine began painting during the same time he painted the fowl. Servants, who were regarded with disdain in the shtetl, are in a sense the scapegoats of society and emblems of exploitation. Their identity is determined by their social role rather than through their own individual personalities. Soutine painted domestics and servants perhaps for the very reason that they were symbolic of emotional object-catharsis. Perhaps by a similar reactive compulsion, he painted Chartres Cathedral; a shtetl Jew would avert his eyes from a church and walk hurriedly past it. He further violated the tenets of shtetl life by painting series after series of Christian ritualistic figures — choir boys, page boys, communicants.

Another painting with a subject and meaning emotionally laden with shtetl-culture significance is the early *Dog and Forks.* The dog was feared *Ill. 3* in the shtetl, regarded as an unpredictable and dangerous beast, and

Soutine, *Dog and Forks,* oil on canvas. Whereabouts unknown

13

associated with violence. Soutine, in his most overtly cruel picture, paints the animal with his stomach gaping open, held apart by human-hand-like forks. Again the artist portrays a subject fraught with an anxiety instilled in his youth. Perhaps in this case the fear or revulsion *was* exorcized; at about this time Soutine posed proudly for a photograph in which he smiles shyly, holding the paw of a small dog.

Ill. 4

The most significant psychological issue related to the fact that Soutine painted animal carcasses is that his primary subjects — beef and fowl — represented sustenance. In the shtetl, the rituals connected with food were of transcending importance. Food, as Howe observes, "became a link between the holy and profane, the community and the person, husband and wife, mother and children. Precisely because of its scarcity, it was a means of *expressing love and releasing anger*. The happiest holidays of the year mean special foods; the holiest, a denial of food."[20] The all-important Jewish dietary concept of "kosher" depends upon killing the animal as quickly, cleanly, and painlessly as possible, immediately removing all excess blood, and using the meat as soon as possible. But Soutine hung the bloody animal up and investigated it. The power of Soutine's art rests upon this driving necessity to *see* the forbidden thing and to paint it.

Soutine himself elucidated his own deepest longings and motivations in an extraordinary comment made to his friend and biographer, Emile Szittya: "'Once I say the village butcher slice the neck of a bird and drain the blood out of it. I wanted to cry out, but his joyful expression caught the sound in my throat.' Soutine patted his throat and continued, 'This cry, I always feel it there. When, as a child, I drew a crude portrait of my professor, I tried to rid myself of this cry, but in vain. When I painted the beef carcass it was still this cry that I wanted to liberate. I have still not succeeded.'"[21]

*   *   *

In 1913, Soutine finished the three year course at Vilna. He had managed during this time to save enough money for a train ticket to France, and he arrived in Paris in July of that year. The painter Pincus Kremegne, who had been at the Vilna Academy with him, was already living in La Ruche ("The Beehive"), the famous rotunda built for the Paris Exposition which was later made into artists' studios. Kremegne escorted Soutine to these ateliers, where at various times Léger, Chagall, Lipchitz, Kisling and Modigliani lived and worked. Modigliani was to become his close friend and supporter, introducing Soutine to his patron and dealer,

Zborowski. Soutine lived here, and at times in another atelier in the Cité Falguière, for the next six years. In spite of the contacts he made with certain avant-garde artists and poets, he enrolled for a brief period in the academic classes conducted by Cormon who, decades earlier, had taught Van Gogh and Toulouse-Lautrec. Soutine's poverty in those first years in Paris was almost unsupportable; it was the kind of gnawing, continual want that can break one's will to work or live. It left a permanent scar on him both physically and emotionally. During this time, he would occasionally obtain work as a porter at the railroad station, and as a ditch digger during the war. In later years, Soutine recounted standing at the counter of a café for hours, hoping that someone would buy him a café crème or sandwich. Stories of his abject poverty and his notorious uncleanliness at this time are legion. The most poignant anecdotes—such as the tales about how Soutine tried to keep armies of bugs away from his bed with pans of kerosene, or how he made a pair of underwear serve as a shirt—testify both to his stubborn tenacity and his ingenuity in the face of hardship. But for Soutine these years were hardly less bitter than earlier times in Lithuania. Certainly he never recalled them as romantic or adventurous; whatever energy was left from his work was devoted to staying alive.

One of the earliest paintings known today is the melancholy *Portrait of a Nurse,* a picture which is more interesting in terms of Soutine's later *Pl. 1* stylistic development than pleasing in itself. The weary expression on the subject's face appears later in Soutine's development—not in the twenties, when his portraits are generally more animated—but in the thirties. This is significant in a broader sense because certain subjects which Soutine chose in these early years disappeared in the subsequent decade, only to surface again at the end of his life. The work has compositional interest, too, in the radical flattening of the figure onto the picture surface, and the manifest inclination to distort forms for expressive effect—the body of the woman surges up and spreads itself out, like an inanimate phantom. This feature was developed in the twenties: see for example Plates 38 and 39. *Still Life with Lemons* belongs to a type *Pl. 2* of early still life which depicts a dark bottle and glass, a plate with an item of food on it, a spoon or fork, and one or two other items, all seen frontally on an upturned table-top. The objects are carefully and somewhat stiffly arranged; the manner in which the edge of the plate meets the bottom of the vase is typical. Cézanne's palette and sustained use of subtle distortions for surface tensions seems to have affected Soutine

Soutine, *Portrait of M. Chauveau,* c. 1917, oil on canvas, 21⅝ x 18⅛″. Photograph courtesy Galerie Charpentier, Paris

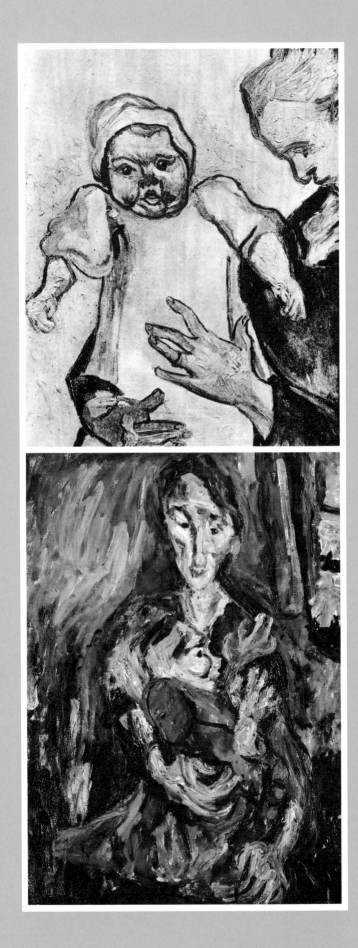

considerably in these early years. The fork is most individually realized. It quivers and trembles as if alive, and anticipates the grasping anthropomorphic utensils encountered in slightly later still lifes.

Soutine painted portraits of fellow artists and of political refugees who lived at La Ruche, as in the portrait of *M. Chauveau*. Here he commences his struggle to transform objective appearance into a world of pervasively convoluted form. His means at this stage is the occasional exaggeration of natural irregularities — the sloping hairline, the high, protruding cheekbone and enlarged ear. The curvilinear gyrations of the background may be interpreted as symbolic of his wish to make real forms take on their potentially free, spontaneous quality. A diagonal composition, which becomes systematic in the landscapes of Céret, determines the ensemble of forms without the use of supporting horizontal or vertical lines. He found a prototype for this distortion in the forms of El Greco, who, according to Kikoine, Soutine then thought of as "the great master."[22] Certainly Soutine must have looked long and hard at El Greco. The inspired stroking in certain of his canvases reveals his homage to the sixteenth century painter. But Soutine's art contains several elements completely foreign to El Greco — the almost grotesque, comic-demonic aura, the world of terror tempered by humor. These have little in common with El Greco's solemn spiritualism or his effort to de-materialize a mundane world. El Greco's exalted, superterrestrial spiritualism could scarcely have shown him how to make a valid art out of the vulgar realities of daily life. The dwarfs of Velasquez, or the "noble, vulnerable, ordinary" portraits of Rembrandt, in the words of David Sylvester,[23] could have encouraged him. But it is especially Van Gogh, also a stranger in France, who furnished the artist with proof that his own native sensibility could find valid expression in painting. For Van Gogh, facing his model, was attentive not only to the superficial particularities but also to the deeper characteristics of personality (often neglected in earlier art) which are clumsy, base, mad or despairing. In his portrait of *Mme. Roulin and Her Child,* Van Gogh rejected the traditional vision of doting maternity and insisted upon expressing awkward helplessness through the child. Soutine took a similar approach in a canvas of 1918 in which he stressed the gracelessness of the gesticulating child. Like Van Gogh, Soutine painted deformed hands which, so much are they distorted, seem not to belong to the figure but to have an independent existence. Both painters represented one figure from the the front and the other in profile, in order to heighten the stiffness of the relationship between

Ill. 5

Ill. 6

Ill. 7

Van Gogh, *Mme. Rouline and Her Child,* 1888, oil on canvas, 25⅝ x 20⅛"

Soutine, *Mother and Child,* c. 1919, oil on canvas, 37 x 28¾". Collection Jean Masurel, Roubaix, France

mother and child. In his portrait, Van Gogh "not only [did] away with the dark shadows of older portraiture," as Meyer Schapiro wrote, but also "with that smoothness of the paint and the represented skin which has been so important in the past."[24] Soutine understood that very well.

Cézanne's influence upon Soutine in these years was less direct than that of Van Gogh, but perhaps it was equally important in determining Soutine's underlying spatial approach. David Sylvester has argued that Cézanne's effect on Soutine gradually became more significant than virtually any other painter, pointing to certain derivations from Cézanne — modeling by color rather than tone, breaking a form into clearly articulated planes, compressing solidity into flatness.[25] Yet only the last characteristic holds for any appreciable body of Soutine's work. Indeed, he did seem to learn a great deal from Cézanne's way of severely constricting and enclosing space within which forms would be flatly imprisoned. In Cézanne the object is tilted upward to become parallel to the picture plane, and specific objects become distorted to accommodate the flattening of the ground. Soutine clearly adopted this approach in his early still lifes, although with far less consistency in the handling of each object. But Soutine would always make spatial compression uniquely meaningful to his own expression, thereby transforming what could have been merely a pictorial device into a supremely personal metaphor. This became Soutine's means of expressing the ineluctable fusion of all form and matter, the identification of form and flesh and pigment which is so basic to his still lifes, landscapes and portraits throughout the twenties.

Another key formal influence is clearly apparent in several pictures made early in 1918. If Soutine gleaned from Cézanne the means of unifying a picture by spatial compression, he learned from Bonnard how to impart a consistent quality of viscosity to the canvas surface. In pictures like *Flowers and Fruit* and *Landscape with Figure* one sees the origin of his membranous pigment-skin. Bonnard showed him how to work the pigment in a "wet" and tightly-knit manner. The strokes are muted but strong, possessed of individual weight and purpose. One of his early Céret landscapes painted in 1919, two years later, reveals a continued experimentation with Bonnard's manner of flecking and spotting paint. This extraordinary painting also embodies the lessons of Van Gogh and Cézanne, the surging vehemence of the former and a version of the latter's constriction of near and far into a narrow, vibrating space. Directly after this seminal work, Soutine arrived at a certain synthesis and began to find his own way.

Pls. 8, 9

Pl. 11

Sometime in 1918 Soutine left Paris, probably for the first time since he had arrived in France, to visit Cagnes. The following year he visited Céret in the Pyrenees, where he later settled in 1919 for about three years. Away from the museums and galleries of Paris — and it must always be remembered how deeply responsive Soutine was to his visual environment — Soutine took great strides forward. Perhaps his dealer, Zborowski, intuitively grasped the potential consequences of sending Soutine away from the art capital, and for this reason supported him at Céret.

The ascendant, quintessential power of Soutine's Céret period work was first made prominent by certain American abstract expressionist painters; consequently this aspect of Soutine's oeuvre came to be widely appreciated and understood through its affinities with the work of the New York School artists. (Similarly, German Expressionism at the turn of the century prompted a renewal of interest in the then neglected artist El Greco.) In his catalog of the Museum of Modern Art's 1950 Soutine exhibition, Monroe Wheeler called attention to the connections between Soutine's Céret work and abstract expressionism, but it was the painter Jack Tworkov who wrote perhaps the most penetrating criticism of the Céret work. Indeed Tworkov's lines now appear to be among the most illuminating critical remarks made in 1950, not only about Soutine at Céret but also about the new American painting. Tworkov wrote that Soutine's painting "technically defies analysis of how to do it. But it is precisely this impenetrability to logical analysis as far as his method is concerned, that quality of the surface which appears as if it had happened rather than as 'made,' which unexpectedly reminds us of the most original section of the new painting in this country. Viewed from the standpoint of certain painters, like De Kooning and perhaps Pollock, about whom there is no reason to imagine any real Soutine influence, certain qualities of composition, certain attitudes toward paint which have gained prestige here as the most advanced painting, are expressed in Soutine in unpremeditated form. These can be summarized as: the way his picture moves towards the edge of the canvas in centrifugal waves filling it to the brim; his completely impulsive use of pigment as a material, generally thick, slow-flowing, viscous, with a sensual attitude toward it, as if it were the primordial material, with deep and vibratory color; the absence of any effacing of the tracks bearing the imprint of the energy passing over the surface. The combined effect is of a full, packed, dense picture of enormous seriousness and grandeur, lacking all embellishment or any concession to decoration."[26]

A word should be added at this point about the problems of dating Soutine's work. In the notes to the Arts Council of Great Britain's Soutine exhibition of 1963, I proposed a chronological scheme which revised Monroe Wheeler's account of Soutine's development, then the most accurate hypothesis. Exception was taken primarily to Wheeler's dating of the Céret period. Before Wheeler's study, writers on Soutine avoided dating Soutine's work altogether or posited dates which were off the mark by a decade or more. Even the brilliant art historian Elie Faure, who knew the artist personally, wrote a little monograph (bibl. 6) rather early in Soutine's career which contains surprising errors in dating paintings which were quite recent at the time. In 1959 the Galerie Charpentier mounted the largest exhibition of Soutine paintings ever organized, but the catalog gave a confused picture of Soutine's chronology. The chronological scheme which I proposed in 1963 was largely based on considerations of style, with certain datings offered provisionally. I hoped that the exhibition and the proposed ascriptions would encourage further study and clarification of Soutine's art at each point in its evolution. This did in fact occur, for while the exhibition was on display in London, an art class under the direction of David Sylvester, who organized the 1963 exhibition, studied the paintings in question and modified several of the dates offered, while generally accepting the proposed scheme. The resultant chronology, altered to account for the many additional or substituted paintings in the present exhibition, serves as a framework for the following commentary.

An early work at Céret presages the psychological quality of the entire Céret production of about 200 canvases. It is the *Reclining Woman*. This *Pl. 10* painting is about *immersion* in the earth, presented almost literally, for the figure seems pressed into the ground, and the folds of her dress are like the creases and grass of the earth. The painting is highly provocative of the qualities of formal immersion and self-immersion which are the root of Soutine's mature work.

Soutine's stylistic development at Céret is best illustrated in his landscapes. Over a period of three years, the forms in these paintings become increasingly convoluted, their axis, for some reason, inclining ever more to the right side of the picture. In 1921 a pervasive convolution of the forms is effected, accompanied by a more upright placement. Thereafter, the pictures become more symmetrical and more calligraphic; the urge toward abstraction diminishes; figure-ground relationships become clarified.

Road of Trees, circa 1919, is a crucial picture in terms of ascertaining *Ills. 8, 9*

Soutine, *Road of Trees,* c. 1919, oil on canvas, 21¼ x 28¾″. Photography courtesy Arts Council of Great Britain

Photograph of road of trees at Céret, 1967, by Maurice Tuchman

the stylistic development of the Céret style. This view of the road leading to the village was done early in the Céret period, and is one of a series of pictures that have rarely been presented in studies of Soutine. A sense of uprootedness prevails here, epitomized in the great yearning of the trees for the edges of the canvas. Blazing red brush strokes are introduced. In the *View of Céret* the vista is spread out laterally, and individual forms *Ill. 10, Pl. 12* consistently incline toward the right. That this seemingly arbitrary inclination may have been suggested by the actual view is indicated by the location photograph. The forms quiver and vibrate and begin to lose a sense *Ill. 11* of mass; modeling begins to yield to calligraphic agitation. The landscapes become increasingly violent and convulsive. The painter's vantage point moves closer to the forms. In a picture such as *Landscape at Céret* *Pl. 13* one aspect of "high" Céret style emerges—the impulsive unobstructed surge of long diagonals to a point of convergence at the upper right. Thus the sense of being close-up is taken a step further, and approaches a sensation of being *inside;* that is, completely immersed in a world of violent sensation. The pictures become airless, the space flat and dense, the textures liquid and thick, the shapes less easily legible and often ecstatic; as, for example, the bursts of foliage in the *Landscape at Céret.* In the Tate *Pl. 14* Gallery's *Landscape,* so intense is the turbulence that only gradually do *Pl. 15* the separate parts—the trees of the foreground, house in the middle distance, and the background hill—come into focus. This is clearly the same view seen in the picture previously mentioned, and their obvious similarity confirms the fact that Soutine was looking very hard at the forms, even while transforming the perception into something almost unrecognizable. Noteworthy too are formal inventions which occur in these pictures in spite of the frenetic haste of their execution. In the Tate picture the foliage at the upper left, which belongs to the foreground tree, neatly parallels the contour of the distant hill; areas belonging to radically separated spatial planes are thus tied to each other. This trait appears again years later in a different type of painting—a portrait—painted in another style; see the similar configuration of hat and shoulder in the *Woman in Red.* Monroe *Pl. 41* Wheeler dates the extraordinary *Hill at Céret* as circa 1919, but its com- *Pl. 16* plex and profuse anthropomorphic forms indicate that it was executed at the high point of Soutine's Céret style. Thomas B. Hess wrote memorably of this anthropomorphism in his response to the picture in 1950: "I see the hill with a house on top, but below, and to the left, I find a hook-nosed witch, a handkerchief tied around her head, holding the collar of a squatting dragon. But the beast's right side is defined by a dark area which now

Soutine, *View of Céret,* c. 1919-20, oil on canvas, 21¼ x 28¾". Collection Nathan Cummings, Chicago

Photograph of landscape at Céret, 1967, by Maurice Tuchman

appears to be a curling-horned steer, drastically foreshortened, rising up to the farmhouse, while below, guarding his eyes with his forearm, a man tumbles backward into the sea. A few minutes later, I might have difficulty in finding some of these forms again. Perhaps the landscape will return, with all its roads, banks of trees, coils of earth, and flying clouds. But the very manipulation of pigment has pried the subject from nature into the personal sensation of terror, violence — and paint . . . Nature is again populated with demi-gods who re-sanctify their ancient myths under the most banal fields or within everyday trees." [27]

A photograph taken in 1967 of the hill at Céret which Soutine painted dozens of times reveals that the actual hill has a gradual slope, not the high steepness we see in the paintings. Soutine made the hill parallel the picture surface to accommodate the urge for immersion. But it also reveals an urge toward abstraction which is completely unexpected in an artist so rooted in the act of perceiving and so conscious of the claims of tradition. Working alone at Céret, Soutine seems to have lost his need for a tradition-based art. He had always felt a kinship with the old masters, as he told Paul Guillaume in 1923. Guillaume cited Soutine's taste for "precursors" of expressionism such as El Greco, Courbet, Tintoretto, Goya and Rembrandt, but Soutine also admired Egyptian and Greek sculpture, and "classical" artists such as Raphael, Corot, Cézanne and Fouquet. Jacques Lipchitz recalls having met Soutine leaving the Louvre one Sunday afternoon. Soutine approached Lipchitz enthusiastically, brandishing a reproduction which he had bought in the museum. "Here," he said, "is the greatest painting in the Louvre." Lipchitz looked at the picture: it was Fouquet's *Portrait of Charles VII*. [28] For Soutine, restraint and discipline were extremely important qualities in the art of the past. I would suggest that it was in part this radical departure from tradition in the Céret pictures that Soutine later came to detest, and which accounts in large part for his determination to find and destroy these works. (In the thirties he demeaned the Céret pictures: "I made them with my fingers!") Tradition afforded him a sort of scaffolding, providing him a base from which to proceed freely, and permitting him to violate certain traditional canons. Analogies of this psychological need are found in his pictures after the "ultimate" Céret landscape. For example, in *Red Roofs, Céret,* there is an almost architectonic scaffolding around the centered image which sets that image down; the trees at both sides of the picture act as brackets for the rising cubistic mass of houses. This stabilizing element allows him to continue painting at a high emotional pitch. But in this and other Céret landscapes

Ills. 12, 13

Ill. 14

Pl. 18

Soutine, *Hill at Céret,* c. 1921, oil on canvas, 29¼ x 21⅝". Collection Perls Galleries, New York

Photograph of hill at Céret, 1967, by Maurice Tuchman

after the *Hill at Céret,* the ferocity of the brushstroking abates, and jagged *Pl. 16*
angularities of linear movement yield to larger, more gracefully curved
rhythms. Pictures like this, of basically architectural motifs, begin to
occur more often now. They appear to be basically expressionistic treat-
ments of scenes first filtered through the eyes of Cézanne or a Cubist
painter. In Tworkov's words, Soutine's "way is to liquefy the building
blocks of Cézanne...."[29]

Some months later, when Soutine again painted the Céret hill, he *Pl. 19*
stepped back, as it were, to allow a greater calm and definition to emerge.
The hill is more legible and is symmetrically flanked by cypresses and
clouds. Instead of a claustrophobic tangle, there now comes a hint of the
characteristic aspect of later pictures at Cagnes — entrance into the landscape, via upward-winding road or stairs.

Soutine made visits to Cagnes in 1922 and 1923; certain pictures fuse
Céret and Cagnes characteristics, as in the *Landscape with Cypresses.* *Pl. 23*
The central zone of bare tree and thicket is clearly Céret in subject and
treatment, but the clear demarcation of spatial zones, the physiognomic
aspect of the architecture (the houses are now anthropomorphic, rather
than the strokes), and the inclusion of a reclining figure are typical of his
Cagnes works. Although the thicket is dense and airless, the entire picture
nevertheless contains an atmospheric quality related to the greater breadth
and expansiveness of Cagnes landscapes.

During the so-called Cagnes period, 1923-25, the artist divided his time
between Cagnes, neighboring villages, and Paris. The phrase "Cagnes
style" is employed to distinguish his work at this stage from later work
in Paris. At Cagnes the palette becomes brighter and more luminous, due
in part to the summer climate of the Midi. An airy, buoyant, fairytale quality typifies mature Cagnes landscapes. More often than not, a large view
of the town, seen from above (not below as at Céret) typifies the Cagnes
style. As noted, the road image serves as a visual entrance into the picture *Pls. 29-32*
forms, as opposed to the striking absence of any possible accessibility
in the Céret works. The sense of fantasy befits this new motif, just as the
dualism of despair-ecstasy is tied to the self-enclosure of Céret motifs.
Energy which had been projected into the brushstroke and pigment becomes transformed into the composing and balancing of shapes.

During the Céret period Soutine's brushstroke carries the weight of
the pictorial drama. In his utter reliance on spontaneous execution, with
its leaning toward the abstract, Soutine in these years most fully embodied
the expressionist vision. The ascendant importance of the individual

Fouquet, *Portrait of Charles VII,* c. 1451, panel painting, 37⅞ x 28⅜". Collection Musée du Louvre. Photograph courtesy Giraudon
Modigliani, *Caryatid,* c. 1912, oil on canvas, 32 x 17¾". Collection Perls Galleries, New York
Kokoschka, *Still Life with Tortoise and Hyacinth,* 1909, oil on canvas, 34¼ x 44⅞"

brushstroke, the singular touch of the painter's hand, is common to the many modern expressionist styles, abstract as well as representational, from Van Gogh through Soutine to the American abstract expressionists. The expressionist stroke is loaded, highly charged and self-assertive. It carries the gesture of the artist in the painting act, and implies the force of body movement, not merely the motion of the wrist, as in Impressionism. The expressionist painter's touch contains in embryo the qualities of his larger expression. It is one of the miracles of art that a mere mark can be so evocative of feeling and sensibility. Thus Van Gogh's stroke seems to burn into canvas with savage but deliberate forcefulness; Rouault's characteristic stroke is like a flagellant's blow, ecstatic and unconstrained; Kokoschka's mark is a seismographic quiver, an exquisitely sensitive recorder of decay and musty glamour; Kandinsky's touch may be dainty or aggressively blunt, thin and spindly, or feverishly explosive, but it is always in unpredictable dynamic flux; Soutine's typical stroke is usually not a line but a fleshy patch, a section of sentient visceral matter. De Kooning's emphatic method, influenced by Soutine, piles one potent charge of paint upon another, implying even more consistently than Soutine a constantly self-generating process.

*　　　*　　　*

The singular approach to portraiture which is present as early as 1916 *Pl. 1, Ill. 5* in *Portrait of a Nurse* and *Portrait of M. Chauveau* remains typical of Soutine throughout his life; basically, it is the distinctive manner in which the figure is placed in the picture field. Subjects are set into their pictorial space with a certain clumsy rigor. They are centrally and frontally positioned. The tendency to a kind of primitive or naive approach is due in part to the example of Soutine's close friend Modigliani. Another indication of Modigliani's influence upon Soutine's figure compositions occurs in the typical Céret portrait, in which a figure is set against a real or imagined hanging drapery, flanked on both sides by empty space, usually in *Ill. 15* distinctly vertical format. Compare Modigliani's *Caryatid* to Soutine's *Pl. 28* *Little Pastry Cook*. Soutine's figures face you and command your attention. Yet they are apparently indifferent to the presence of the artist. While Soutine "projected" himself into his portraits, there is still much individual characterization in these works. A photograph of one of Soutine's models, the *Farm Girl,* taken at Cagnes twenty-six years after she posed for Soutine, still reveals a remarkable likness. There is little trace in Soutine's portraits of the typically modern dialogue between painter and model which is so characteristic, for example, of the early portraits of Oskar Kokoschka who, apart from Soutine, is probably the most original portrait painter of the century. Soutine's personages *pose* purely and simply; they do not develop the freer tendency signaled by Van Gogh's portraits. The models of Soutine pose in a "classical" manner. Whereas the subjects of Renaissance masters are represented in an ennobling manner, symbolizing their occupation or social position, those of Soutine project an awkwardness, a sense of prolonged constraint, as in old daguerreotypes. Soutine's admiration for Egyptian sculpture may be a precedent for the sense in his work of tension resulting from movement become frozen and still. At first glance, Soutine's models are seemingly free in their life space, but they are flattened and distorted, spread out and hung up. Their flesh is metamorphosed into purely colored paste, its viscous surface often of the same textural consistency as the background or surrounding space. All is flesh, all as if flesh were grafted onto flesh. (Roald Dahl's short story, "Skin," features "Chaim Soutine" tattooing a portrait with "that twisted, tortured, quality" all over a friend's back—a brilliant metaphor of Soutine's actual approach.[30])

Ills. 16, 17

Between 1918 and 1923, when he reached the age of thirty, Soutine painted several self portraits. The most famous of these, in the collection of Henry Pearlman, is characterized by its predominant bright reds and greens, reminiscent of a famous Van Gogh self portrait. The boldness of the color contrasts define the principal forms: the oval of the head is placed in the center of the picture, and the pose, directly frontal, with a fixed gaze, gives an impression of rigid concentration. Soutine's next self portrait, painted about 1920, is an image of immobility and pain. As in other portraits, the model is placed, or pressed, against a wall-hanging. The treatment of the flesh is the same as of the clothing and curtain. The impression of a central mass is augmented by the rigidness of the pose, with the arms pinned against the sides, a surprising posture for a self portrait. A void encloses the figure; the scarf around the neck accentuates the sense of restriction. An eerie sense of dislocation is suggested by the head and artist's left arm: they seem to be severed from the torso. As in all his self portraits, the hands are eliminated. This is a significant fact in the light of the importance which the hands have in his portraits of others. Soutine's

Pl. 5

Ill. 1

own hands, remarkably slender and delicate, impressed those who knew him, including Modigliani (see Modigliani's portrait of Soutine in Washington's National Gallery).

Ills. 19, 20

Soutine's last self portrait, again in tones of red and green, was started at Céret and finished at Cagnes in 1923. The artist clearly had trouble *Pl. 34* resolving the picture to his satisfaction, perhaps because it is a pitiless, ruthless work, ridden with self-contempt. The artist's left arm has been painted out, sliced away in an abrupt manner. A series of gyrating rhythms was added later to widen the back of the figure; these green strokes, curiously unmatched to the original yellow of the coat, have the hue of Cagnes painting. Rarely did Soutine come so close to caricature as in this work; for while caricature seizes on a few salient features for exaggeration, Soutine typically remakes the entire face, exaggerating *everything*, so far as is possible, rather than selecting a few features in accordance with a witty formula. But in the last self portrait Soutine scornfully stretches the nose, widens the ear, diminishes the eyes and makes the lips monstrously pendulous.

Soutine almost always painted the figure from a disconcertingly short distance, and always head on, frontally, except for an extraordinary series of Céret portraits of praying men. The fully frontal or three-quarter view *Pls. 25-26* is of course more conducive to a painterly approach, in contrast to the calligraphic portraits of Kokoschka, which are so often in profile (i.e., *Herwarth Walden*). The act of supplication, however, is particularly suited to a profile view, because a praying person is detached from the viewer. In Soutine's painting the entire figure is transmogrified into a red, flame-like shape, recalling the common shtetl vision of God as a noncorporeal burning presence.

In this series as well as in other Céret portrait paintings, Soutine strives for an all-pervasive unity. To this end he employs an homogenous surface texture and intuitively invents a system of deformations, a lexicon of simple angular forms which impart to the face and body the same expressiveness. Fewer portraits than landscapes were painted at Céret, and these generally have a sense of a landscape approach; the praying figures are like some organic form threatened and bent by the forces of nature.

Corresponding to the sharper and more angular style of this period, the models at Céret are almost always men; at Cagnes (1923-25), most of the portraits are female, conforming to the curvilinear flowing rhythms basic to the style of this period. At Céret, angularity attends the detachmen and rigidity of Soutine's models; man is seen as a symbol of nature.

Soutine, *Farm Girl,* c. 1921, oil on canvas, 31½ x 17½". Collection Dr. and Mrs. Harry Bakwin, New York

Photograph of Soutine model, Cagnes, 1959. Courtesy Paris Match

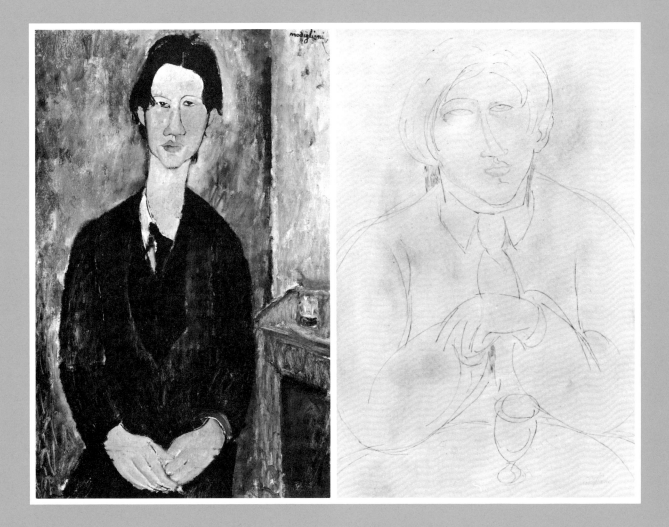

This identification of man and nature is already evident in the 1918 *Self Portrait* where the clothing resembles a volcanic flow. At Cagnes, the exact opposite holds; landscape becomes secondary to portraiture both in production and quality, and landscape takes on consistently anthropomorphic qualities — houses look like faces.

Pl. 5

The *Woman in Red,* one of Soutine's most famous paintings, was dated circa 1922 by Monroe Wheeler; the smooth rounded curves of the picture suggest, however, a greater distance from the angularity characteristic of Céret. This is one of the first paintings with a large, daring elliptical shape, anticipating the still lifes of the mid-twenties. The picture has been cleaned since it was reproduced in Wheeler, revealing that an important portion of the hat had been over-painted, almost certainly not by the artist. The retouching had drastically altered the design of the entire canvas by breaking the rhythmic flow from hat through chair and arms, and by weakening the forceful oppositions in the face.

Pl. 41

Pls. 59, 60

Soutine's attraction to uniformed figures and to dead animals was simultaneous. Interest in both types of subjects was awakened and declined at the same time, from 1923 to about 1928. In the great still lifes, enormous quarters of beef hang, entrails exposed, the internal substance of their life analysed and painted with great care. Pheasants, geese and other deplumed fowl are strung up by their necks. Large ominous face-like rayfish hover behind tables. Some critics have insisted that Soutine wanted to project the spectacle of putrid flesh out of morbid interest in decay. But a look at a painting like Kokoschka's *Still Life with Tortoise and Hyacinth* — an image of mould, a veritable emblem of nausea — points up how far removed Soutine's work is from such romantic morbidity. The fascination of flesh for Soutine resides not at all in *Weltschmerz,* but in its character as the primary element, the primordial material. His passion is for the texture and color of flesh. The dense, rich color-pigment of the *Beef* is of the same order as the *Girl in Pink* and is also related to the Céret landscape vision. Sometimes Soutine's portraits also resemble certain still lifes in the way the form is flattened and stretched out at both sides, as though the figure were being prepared for anatomical dissection.

Pls. 65, 66

Pls. 69-71, 62-64

Ill. 20

Pl. 45

The true analogy between the twenties still lifes and figure paintings lies in Soutine's choice of uniformed figures. Uniforms are interesting visually and significant spiritually. Uniforms undoubtedly appealed to Soutine by their unified tonality and less varied textures than "civilian" garments. And the effect of the uniform is to hide individuality, to de-personalize, to cover uniqueness with anonymity. In Soutine's portraits of costumed fig-

Pls. 35, 46, 49-52

ures the uniform serves as a sort of artificial skin, an extension, or analogy, of flesh. He sought to translate both materials into a membrane of oil pigment, for him a sort of protoplasmic source of all things. Except on one occasion, when Soutine painted a professional model, he never painted a nude. And in this work (reproduced Wheeler p. 92, see bibl. 78), the nude woman stands so self-consciously, her posture of abashed timidity is so painfully obvious, that one is touched by the artist's own embarrassment. There is great irony in the fact that an artist whose brushstroke is so sensual, and whose method depends so completely on the presence of the model, should shrink from depicting the female body. But it is understandable in the light of the shtetl's severe injunction against witnessing nakedness. By painting uniforms Soutine avoided these anxieties and could work impasto as if it were living clay.

Painting in series became more necessary to Soutine in the "Paris period," 1925-29. Subjects became more difficult to find and they took on greater significance to the artist. He would not paint "variations on a theme," however. His concern was to get the image right, no matter how many trials it took. Some subjects were painted twenty times, and there is startingly little significant formal variation to be found in such series. The difference is in their quality, a matter usually of the vivid, febrile *aliveness* of the surface.

Sometimes Soutine was led to a motif by the painting of an earlier master. Chardin's *Still Life with Rayfish* in the Louvre inspired Soutine to make at least three paintings of this eerily human-like fish in 1924-25.

Ill. 22

Ill. 21

Rembrandt's *Beef Carcass,* also in the Louvre, led Soutine to install a carcass in his studio at Rue du Mont St. Gothard. He had to set up a model. Once Soutine made an overnight train trip to Amsterdam just to see Rembrandt's *The Jewish Bride,* then went directly back to his Paris studio and tried to paint it from memory. He could not do it, and destroyed his attempt. The choice and position of both these subjects, rather than any specific stylistic feature, comprised the essential influence on Soutine. These works are not "interpretations" of Rembrandt or Chardin, nor are they paintings of paintings as, for example, are some of Picasso's late paintings after Velasquez. They are singular in modern art as candid acknowledgments of older work. Their modernity, compared to their seventeenth and eighteenth century prototypes, rests in their great size (the beefs are among the largest Soutines), the striking vibrancy (a result of many daring contrasts of pure tones) and the prevailing sensuousness of pigment, even into background areas.

*   *   *

It is now possible to present a full view of Soutine's manner of working, drawing upon the observations of a dozen personal acquaintances of the artist. While Soutine's way of painting changed over the years, certain consistencies remained. Always, the subject was his inspiration. As time went on, fewer subjects presented themselves to him; longer were the periods of lassitude and dejection.

In Paris during the twenties he would search the poultry shops with a friend for a particular chicken, one with a "long neck and blue skin." His friends recount how Soutine pronounced the word 'blue' with savor, almost gluttony—"You know, a beautiful 'bellue'." On one occasion, the poulterer offered him a fat chicken, out of sympathy for Soutine's apparent poverty, but Soutine insisted on buying an emaciated fowl: "I want a very lean chicken with a long neck and flaccid skin." Finally, much to the poulterer's bewilderment, he found the wretched specimen he wanted. On the street he held up the bird admiringly and said, "I'm going to hang it up by the beak with a nail. In a few days it should be perfect."[31] Another *Ill. 23* friend of Soutine's recalls going with him to a butcher to buy a calf's head and explaining to the butcher why he had to choose it himself. "You do understand," he said, "I want a calf's head of distinction."[32] The problems posed by obtaining live human models were of course somewhat greater. There is a famous story about how Soutine became enraptured with the wife of a proud peasant, how he implored the poor woman to pose for him, persuaded friends to vouch for the purity of his motive, and finally succeeded. But he failed to convince her husband. Finally, after days of pleading and threatening, he managed to obtain the woman's service.[33] The act of pursuing, locating, seizing and fixing the model before him is analogous to the passion with which he finally painted the subject.

When the sought-after subject was positioned, he would simply stare at it for a long time before picking up charcoal or brush. In the words of his mistress, "Mlle. Garde," "Soutine set off in search of any trees worth painting. At last he found a subject. As usual, he looked at the subject at least ten times before deciding to paint it. He went, came back, returned and made so much commotion running back and forth between our house and the trees that it aroused the attention of the police who thought he must be a dangerous madman."[34] He could not bear to have anyone watch him while he painted, nor did he allow anyone to see his work until it was finished and judged acceptable by him. Mlle. Garde tells us, "He was so bashful about his unfinished work that he would go so far as to write to me, when we were apart, to tell me not to look at the paintings in progress

in his studio."[35] For a time in the thirties, Soutine had a chauffeur. This man told Pierre Courthion in 1960 that when Soutine worked in the country he would place himself with the easel so that no one could be behind him. In painting the *Tree at Vence,* for example, he lodged himself in a corner. Because of the security this spot offered him — as well as the fact that to him this particular tree was, in his words, "like a cathedral"[36]— he made a large series of paintings of it.

Pls. 72, 73

Once started, Soutine generally worked in a frenzy of exaltation oblivious to the weather or the human needs of his model. (Once a thunderous cloudburst drenched both him and his subject but he forbade her to move and nearly finished the painting during the storm.) It is said that one day, in a fury of painting, he dislocated his thumb. Monroe Wheeler tells us that "he kept his brushes immaculate, one for each nuance of color and each magnitude of brush-stroke, beginning with about forty of them, and discarding them on the floor as fast as he used them."[37] A lady painter who once was privileged to watch him in his studio recounts that, "he flung the colors onto the canvas like poisonous butterflies."[38] Another report of Soutine working on the beef series in 1925 has it that he "threw himself from a distance *bang bang bang* at the canvas."[39] "He worked intensely until he reached a state of exhaustion," reports the sculptor Chana Orloff. "The rapidity of his execution was incredible. He would harbor an idea for months, and then take up his brushes, abandoning them only when the canvas was finished."[40] A model who posed for Soutine early in his life in Paris described Soutine at work: "He turned as red as a crayfish, opening his eyes wide, and his beautiful fingers rubbed his throat and caressed his face. The emotion seemed to stimulate a sense of the colors in him, and he muttered incomprehensible words between his clenched teeth."[41]

"It all depends," Soutine said, "on the way you mix color, catch it, place it."[42] Soutine's concern with getting the image exactly as he felt it, and his relative lack of interest in fitting the image within the picture field, is illustrated in the *Portrait of a Child,* painted over colorfully patterned linoleum; he was able to work directly on the inflected field without distraction, an almost inconceivable approach for any other modern artist. This single-minded concern for his own projected image is reflected in his choice and use of canvas. It is well known that Soutine, beginning in the early Paris years, would search the flea market to buy old, worthless paintings, that he would scour, clean and then paint over them. At first this may have been partly for economic reasons. But he maintained this habit even when he could afford new canvases. Jokingly, perhaps, he men-

Ill. 24

Rembrandt, *Beef Carcass,* 1655, oil on wood, 37 x 26⅜". Collection Musée du Louvre. Photograph courtesy Vizzavona, Paris

Chardin, *Still Life with Rayfish,* c. 1728, oil on canvas, 44⅞ x 57½". Collection Musée du Louvre. Photograph courtesy Vizzavona, Paris

tioned that "this vandalism, which makes me eliminate a bad painting, obliges me to make a masterpiece."[43] He may have felt that the old bed of paint was a better receiver of the textures he would add to it. He used to say of the cleaned surface of the old canvases: "I like to paint on something smooth. *I like my brush to slide.*"[44]

A number of Soutine paintings were photographed in 1933. These photographs provide direct evidence that Soutine tacked his canvases to the wall, only summarily marking off the edge, which allowed him to cut down or enlarge the field of his painting after the image was realized. *Ill. 25* He had no real understanding of scale. In this deficiency, Kikoine's remark that no painter from the shtetl could ever completely overcome the absence of a pictorial tradition is relevant. Soutine, however, did compose in a fresh and often a sophisticated manner in regard to the *inner* harmonies of the image, not in relationship of the image to the picture frame. In this way, he is unlike most important twentieth century artists, to whom the entire canvas surface is of crucial concern, so that inflections of the field are metaphors of world-space. The supreme paradox in Soutine's work is that, while above all it is born in the perceiving process, it is not an art meant to be observed. That Soutine himself felt this way is strongly suggested by the fact that he never had any paintings on his wall, not his own or anyone else's, not even reproductions of old masters. His canvases were carelessly strewn and stacked, unstretched, in a closet or locked room. Soutine's art was made from urgent inner necessity. It demands to be similarly experienced, not dispassionately contemplated. Soutine himself could not be dispassionate about his own work, as is indicated by his reaction to one of his own paintings, a portrait of a small girl. He attempted to retrieve this work from a dealer in order to repaint it. When the dealer refused to relinquish it, Soutine grudgingly acquiesced, but implored him, "Please don't look too closely at her feet. She is very poor and her shoes need mending."[45] He thought of the personages in his own art as real, living additions to the natural world. Soutine's paintings should not be considered as examples in art history, or as a search for formal solutions to painterly problems. As much as it often relates to older painting, Soutine's art is eminently not *about* art.

Szittya relates that accomplishing a painting always made Soutine sad.[46] The artist apparently could not conceive of his work as having any real value, but he stridently maintained that, even so, it was better than that of any other contemporary painter, "better than Modigliani, Chagall and Kremegne. Someday I will destroy my canvases but they

are too cowardly to do it."[47] He lacerated and destroyed many of his paintings with the same frenzy that attended their creation. Sometimes he would lay out a series of works on the floor, as if they were on exhibition, study them for hours and then seize a knife and plunge it into several works. He would destroy works immediately if anyone expressed any reservation about their quality, or if the viewer happened to say that they reminded him of another artist. Destroying his Céret paintings became for Soutine an actual diversion, strangely entertaining to him, enjoyable like the savagery of the wrestling matches which he regularly attended. He would install his mistress in a café, go in search of a Céret picture he had heard some dealer owned, exchange with him a new picture for the old one, and ritually, happily, destroy it.

It should be noted that complete destruction was not always the intention of his attacks, except that destruction vented upon the Céret pictures. Sometimes Soutine would lacerate a picture simply to cut out the portion of canvas he liked. In a picture of a reclining female, for example, Soutine focused upon the poignant expression of weariness in the model's face — a weariness prompted by Soutine's forcing her not to move for hours until she practically fainted. Having elicited the exact mood he had wanted, Soutine hastily painted the face and figure. Later, when he displayed the picture, he was dismayed when a viewer did not comment on the enervated look in the model's eyes, and he promptly slashed away almost all of the canvas, save for the face of the model.[48] In his overriding concern with the image (as opposed to the relationship of image and field), Soutine was absolutely opposed to virtually all important twentieth century art. Soutine's desire was almost exclusively to make the perception a concrete reality.

Acute observers have noticed that often Soutine's lacerations were confined to the edges of the canvas, leaving the central image intact. (In practically all of Soutine's still lifes and portraits, and in many of his landscapes, the forms are centrally located in the picture field.) René Gimpel records that Soutine told him that he often lacerated his canvases "so that the dealers may recanvas them, as after the recanvasings they are more beautiful than he could make them."[49] And Szittya relates that once Soutine "discovered nine of his canvases that someone had recovered from the trash bins, repaired in a masterly fashion and carefully resuscitated. They seemed newer than when Soutine had destroyed them. It is said that he found them 'not so bad' and that he winked slyly."[50] Judging from the accounts now available, it appears that Soutine did not

mind if the composition was altered to some degree, provided that there was no tampering with his brushstroke. This sent him into a rage.

All observers of Soutine's work point out that he almost never sketched or made drawings. Mlle. Garde, who lived with him for four years, tells us that he "never even drew mechanically, on paper napkins, as many painters do," and that he always began by "putting paint directly on the canvas without any preliminary drawing."[51] Of course Soutine was rarely *seen* painting by anyone. Now evidence has emerged that indicates that Soutine did sketch on canvas, at least sometimes, probably preparatory to painting. Jean Leymarie published three such charcoal on canvas sketches in 1963, and dated them 1937-41.[52] The style of these works, however, bears no relationship at all to his painting of that time: they are certainly connected to Soutine's portraits of about 1923.

The drawings reveal that Soutine was a draughtsman of elegance, originality and unusual intensity. Now come to light after perhaps forty-five years, their existence raises the question of the role of calligraphy in Soutine's overwhelmingly painterly oeuvre. These drawings appear at the time when Soutine's work takes on airiness and lightness and certain fanciful delicate qualities completely unheralded in his earlier work. The Cagnes period is characterized, indeed, by a shift from heavy, slashing stroking to curvilinear, rhythmical gesticulations. Beginning at Cagnes and until about 1929 there exists in Soutine's work an alternative approach (not yet discussed by critics) to the heavily impasted but fluid surface so typical of the artist. An excellent example of this other manner is the *Pheasants,* which is as ephemeral and subtle as it is sophisticated in its *Pl. 69* design. When Soutine *draws* more and *attacks* the canvas less, he makes more elaborate compositions, employing a greater number of objects. Noteworthy too is the fact that in these more sophisticated works, the painter distances himself from the objects: they are small in relation to the total canvas surface. Beginning at least when he left Céret, Soutine was aware of the conflicting demands made by each approach, and of the limitations inherent in each. (His later enmity toward Modigliani is interesting in this regard, for once he scornfully declared that his deceased friend's work "was not painting."[53]) If Soutine captured the raw vigor of lines and planes swarming on the picture surface, he lost the elegance of rarefied, aloof formal organization, and vice versa. A synthesis was occasionally reached: in the *Woman in Red,* for instance, a controlled, searching outline encloses an ecstatic fluidity of direct stroking. *Pl. 41*

*　　*　　*

Dr. Albert C. Barnes' famous acquisition in 1923 of scores of Soutine paintings (estimates vary from 50 to 100), as well as subsequent purchases of Soutine's work by other collectors the following year, created a demand for his paintings which continued throughout his life. After this Soutine never again had to worry about financial deprivation. He avoided the haunts of his earlier Paris years and broke relations with most of his previous friends. He developed odd fetishes, such as buying dozens of hats of exactly the same shape and gray color. He apparently came to believe that clothing had almost supernatural powers. Once during the Occupation, the Jewish artist was seen strolling nonchalantly in a Paris street. Alarmed, a friend stopped him and warned him of the danger of being recognized and apprehended, but Soutine tried to assure his friend that he couldn't be recognized because he was wearing a new blue hat.[54] Although Soutine had a full, thick shock of hair, he lived in mortal fear of losing it and went so far as to engage the services of a nun who visited him regularly to massage and treat it with a special tonic. A friend recalls that on one occasion his anxiety grew to such proportions that he clapped a raw egg on his head and covered it with a hat: he had heard that this was a remedy for baldness. Soutine always had "hydrophobia," as Paul Guillaume humorously wrote in 1923, although his seeming aversion to bathing was actually owing in part to his fear of mechanical instruments. Mlle. Garde tells us that some months after he had moved into a modern apartment house, he hadn't had a single bath because he didn't know how to work the water heater.[55]

Soutine also had phobias which were much sadder and more serious. He once told Henri Serouya that he was afraid to deposit money in a bank because when he went there he would be overcome by a terrifying conviction that the uniformed guard was going to creep up behind and strangle him as he stood before the teller's window.[56] A still more disturbing story concerns the illness which Soutine suffered when he found, in an old discarded tin, a piece of ham he had thrown out. Soutine, who suffered from ulcers all his life, imagined that the other part of the meat, which he had cooked and eaten days before, was now rotting in his stomach as it did in the garbage and that it would soon poison him.[57]

Pl. 55 Around 1929 Soutine's palette dims noticeably; the nervous heat of his color cools down. Even when, as in *Young Woman in Red,* he employs the red-blue combination — so typically French at first glance, but actually alien to the calculated restraint of French painters in its high saturation — the effect is one of emotional diminution, of resonance and sonority. Accompanying this shift toward a more harmonious, if less daring, chromatic homogeneity, is a blurring of the edges of shapes. The outlines of the figures now do not have that earlier quality of searching and exploration. This is often reflected in the facial characterizations of the models, as timidity and passiveness replaces the more animated or anguished expressions of earlier subjects. One thinks of the paintings of the thirties as figure paintings, not as portraits. Rarely do the later figures confront us directly. For the most part, they do not gesticulate, but stand or lie inertly, their hands at their sides, or supporting the head. *Pls. 75, 77, 78* They are tired. Their eyes are veiled or downcast. At times one has the *89, 90* sense that the later subjects *indicate* their feelings with identifiable facial *79-81* mannerisms, rather than having been conjured into life by the painter's all-over inventive, ambiguous and impulsive stroking. To be sure, Soutine chose different kinds of subjects. In the twenties the servants he portrayed were those of the great Parisian night clubs and hotels, "characters" like those encountered in George Orwell's book of the same period, *Down and Out in Paris and London.* In the thirties, however, Soutine selected domestics in bourgeois homes, simpler people, less ambitious and striving, and also less scarred by exploitation. Their garments are not the bright pure colors of uniformed figures on public display but the less assertive shades of household clothing. Soutine turns away from painting dead animals and makes pictures of sheep, donkeys and pigs. The characteristic tone in pictures beginning in the early thirties is sadness. The surface of Soutine's work now is often filmy (his attraction toward Courbet begins now). The exacerbated charge imbuing each thrust of paint becomes diffuse and thinned. Correspondingly, the shapes are no longer immersed in a dense field, so that near and far become one; now they *lie on* the "ground"; they repose or float on the canvas surface. Again this is reflected in an interesting way in the figure paintings. His models now rest on the ground; they are not pressed into it as before. They may stand between two flanking shapes, instead of being pinned up against a drapery like a hanging fowl. Consonant with the quieter mood of landscapes of the early thirties, and with the increased distance between painter and subject, is an alignment of forms into the middle-ground so that often they are encased above and below by areas of sky and ground roughly equal in size. Thus an image of the thirties is typically bracketed *Pls. 84, 85, 87-89* within four flanking areas.

In a series of landscapes painted between 1936 and the end of his life, Soutine appears to have held himself at a distance in order to paint a broader, more grandiose vision. The art of the thirties had aspired toward a state of timelessness and permanence. In this final series, Soutine aims for an expression of majesty. These are not tactile responses to the dynamics of nature, involved with constant flux, immersion and self-generation, as was true earlier. These landscapes are more legible, organized, calligraphic and lyrical than the earlier work of the thirties. Some of the landscapes are reduced to focus on two children, a small boy

Pls. 87, 88 and girl holding hands, perhaps on their return from school. A series of this theme, made in the late thirties, is unprecedented for its faintly anecdotal nature and its distinct air of gentle, sweet pathos. In such

Pl. 76 images as individual children or mother and child together, Soutine returns at the end of his life to themes not touched on since his first years in Paris. Often one senses in these late works a yearning for a new, safe childhood. The long receding road in many of them implies a heartsick loneliness. In these portrayals a new stylistic element is introduced, the darting flick which delineates foliage and suggests motion. In place of the earlier brushstroke, which implied the involvement of the entire body in the painting act, there is now the feeling that the stroke comes from the wrist. The sentient visceral patch becomes a tensely charged arabesque. Perhaps in these late works Soutine again attempted to resolve the linear-painterly dichotomy. There are, then, profound differences between Soutine's early and late manners. But it must be understood that, regardless of the period, Soutine's "hand is the dancer, following the rhythm of the disturbances of the soul."[58]

From 1931 to 1935 Soutine spent his summers near Chartres at the country chateau of patrons. His production declined sharply in this time. The periods of waiting for inspiration became ever longer. He continued his wandering in search of the right landscape, the right model. Mlle. Garde lived with him from 1936 until 1939. She relates that Soutine would hunt for four-leaf clovers for hours on end.

Under the German Occupation, Soutine, as a registered Jew, was forced to take refuge outside Paris in Champigny-sur-Veuldre and other small provincial towns. Several times he was forced to flee from one sanctuary to another when discovery by the Nazis threatened him. His stomach ulcer became more painful and violent attacks of indigestion became more frequent. In August of 1943 he suffered a severe rupture of the ulcer. Because of the dangers of the Occupation, much time was lost in removing him to a Paris clinic. Soutine died during the operation on August 9, 1943.

FOOTNOTES

1 Mark Zborowski and Elizabeth Herzog, *Life is With People,* New York, Schocken, 1962, p. 79.

2 Letter by Kikoine in Raymond Cogniat, *Soutine,* Paris, Editions du Chêne, 1945, p. 29.

3 Chana Orloff, "Mon ami Soutine," *Preuves* (Paris), November 1951, p. 18.

4 Cogniat, *loc. cit.*

5 Henri Serouya, Soutine, (1960), unpublished typescript in French, p. 16. Translation of this and other sections by Jane Livingston.

6 *Loc. cit.*

7 Zborowski, *op. cit.,* p. 411.

8 *Ibid.,* p. 301.

9 Abraham J. Heschel, "The Eastern European Era in Jewish History," *Yivo Annual of Jewish Social Science,* New York, 1946, p. 1.

10 *Loc. cit.*

11 Alfred Kazin, *Selected Short Stories of Sholom Aleichem,* New York, 1950, preface.

12 Zborowski, *op. cit.,* p. 413.

13 Irving Howe and Eliezer Greenberg, eds., *A Treasury of Yiddish Stories,* Cleveland and New York, Meridian, 1958, p. 8.

14 Bible, O.T., A. V. English, Apocrypha, Wisdom of Solomon, Chapter 15:5,6.

15 Zborowski, *op. cit.,* pp. 312-313.

16 *Ibid.,* pp. 316-317.

17 *Ibid.,* p. 339.

18 Serouya, *op. cit.,* p. 49.

19 Zborowski, *op. cit.,* pp. 393-394.

20 Howe, *op. cit.,* p. 11.

21 Emile Szittya, *Soutine et son temps,* Paris, La Bibliothèque des Arts, 1955, pp. 107-108. Translation of this and other sections by Jane Livingston.

22 Cogniat, *op. cit.,* p. 29.

23 David Sylvester, *Chaim Soutine,* London, The Arts Council, 1963, p. 12 [bibl. 119].

24 Meyer Schapiro, *Van Gogh,* New York, Abrams, 1951, p. 18.

25 Sylvester, *op. cit.,* p. 7.

26 Jack Tworkov, "The Wandering Soutine," *Art News,* vol. 49, no. 7, part 1, November 1950, p. 31.

27 Thomas B. Hess, *Abstract Painting,* New York, Viking, 1951, pp. 69-70.

28 Told to the author in 1958 by Professor Meyer Schapiro and subsequently by Jacques Lipchitz.

29 Tworkov, *op. cit.,* p. 31.

30 Roald Dahl, "Skin," in *Someone Like You,* New York, Dell, 1965, pp. 91-106.

31 Michel Georges-Michel, *Les Peintres que j'ai connus,* Paris, Fayard, 1954, pp. 177-178.

32 René Gimpel, *Diary of an Art Dealer,* New York, Farrar, Strauss and Giroux, 1966, p. 377.

33 Monroe Wheeler. *Soutine,* New York, Museum of Modern Art, 1950, pp. 79, 81 [bibl. 77].

34 "My Years with Soutine," as told by 'Mademoiselle Garde' to Michel Ragon, in *The Selective Eye,* p. 146 [bibl. 24].

35 *Ibid.,* p. 145.

36 Pierre Courthion, *Soutine,* unpublished typescript, (1960), p. 51.

37 Wheeler, *op. cit.,* p. 75.

38 Szittya, *op. cit.,* p. 38.

39 Paulette Jourdain as quoted by Courthion, *op. cit.,* p. 44.

40 Orloff, *op. cit.,* p. 20.

41 Szittya, *op. cit.,* p. 45.

42 Marcellin Castaing and Jean Leymarie, *Soutine,* New York, Abrams, 1963, p. 32 [bibl. 31].

43 Orloff, *loc. cit.*

44 Courthion, *loc. cit.*

45 Told to the author by Max Kaganovitch in January, 1963.

46 Szittya, *op. cit.,* p. 38.

47 *Ibid.,* pp. 46-47.

48 Serouya, *op. cit.,* p. 99.

49 Gimpel, *op. cit.,* p. 375.

50 Szittya, *op. cit.,* p. 103.

51 Garde, *op. cit.,* p. 145.

52 Castaing and Leymarie, *op. cit.,* p. 34.

53 Orloff, *op. cit.,* p. 17.

54 *Ibid.,* p. 21.

55 Garde, *op. cit.,* p. 144.

56 Serouya, *op. cit.,* p. 41.

57 *Loc. cit.*

58 Tworkov, *op. cit.,* p. 62.

Photograph of Soutine's last palette, 14⅜ x 11⅝". Collection Museum of Modern Art, New York, gift of Pierre Loeb

Dr. and Mrs. Harry Bakwin, New York

Mr. and Mrs. Sydney R. Barlow, Beverly Hills

Mr. and Mrs. John A. Beck, Houston

Mr. and Mrs. Michael Bennahum, New York

Mrs. Andrew Best, London

Mr. and Mrs. Sidney F. Brody, Los Angeles

Comdr. Sir Michael Culme-Seymour, Bt., London

Nathan Cummings, Chicago

Mr. and Mrs. Otto Edler, London

Mr. and Mrs. Herman Elkon, New York

Mr. and Mrs. Henry David Epstein, New York

Mr. and Mrs. David Finkle, New York

Mr. and Mrs. Henry F. Fischbach, New York

Joseph H. Hazen, New York

Alfred Hitchcock, Los Angeles

Dr. Lucien Kléman, Paris

Mrs. Cecil Blaffer Hudson, Houston

Mrs. H. Harris Jonas, New York

Andras Kalman, London

Dr. and Mrs. Norman F. Laskey, Mt. Kisco, New York

Mr. and Mrs. Irving Levick, Buffalo, New York

Mr. and Mrs. S. J. Levin, Miami Beach

Pierre Lévy, Troyes, France

Dr. and Mrs. Paul Todd Makler, Philadelphia

Mrs. Oscar Miestchaninoff, New York

Miss Carol Campbell Owen, Houston

Mr. and Mrs. Henry Pearlman, New York

Mrs. Sybil H. Perry, New Haven, Connecticut

Mr. and Mrs. Gregor Piatigorsky, Los Angeles

The Ritter Foundation, New York

Edward G. Robinson, Beverly Hills

Edmond Safra, Geneva

Mrs. Margaret Sangster, Hoylake, Cheshire, England

Mrs. Evelyn Sharp, New York

Dr. and Mrs. Howard D. Sirak, Columbus, Ohio

J. Spreiregen, London

Mr. and Mrs. Caleb Steinberg, Denver

Mr. and Mrs. Donald S. Stralem, New York

Lee Vandervelde, Los Angeles

Mr. and Mrs. Lew R. Wasserman, Beverly Hills

Mrs. Lloyd Bruce Wescott, Rosemont, New Jersey

Mr. and Mrs. Rodney L. White, New York

Richard S. Zeisler, New York

The Baltimore Museum of Art

The Art Institute of Chicago

The Cleveland Museum of Art

The Metropolitan Museum of Art, New York

The Minneapolis Institute of Arts

Musée d'Art Moderne de la Ville de Paris

The Museum of Modern Art, New York

The Phillips Collection, Washington, D.C.

Portland Art Museum

Stedelijk Museum, Amsterdam

The Tate Gallery, London

Galerie Beyeler, Basel

M. Knoedler and Co., Inc., New York

Marlborough-Gerson Gallery, Inc., New York

Perls Galleries, New York

E. and A. Silberman Galleries, New York

Galerie André Urban, Paris

CATALOG OF THE EXHIBITION

February 20–April 14, 1968

1 *Portrait of a Nurse* c. 1916, oil on canvas, 25½ x 19½" Los Angeles County Museum of Art

2 *Still Life with Lemons* c. 1916, oil on canvas, 25¾ x 21½" Mr. and Mrs. Irving Levick, Buffalo, New York

3 *Flowers and Fish* c. 1917, oil on canvas, 25½ x 19⅜" Perls Galleries, New York

4 *Spotted Vase* c. 1917, oil on canvas, 25⅝ x 18" Andras Kalman, London

5 *Self Portrait* c. 1918, oil on canvas, 21½ x 18" Mr. and Mrs. Henry Pearlman, New York

6 *Red Gladioli* c. 1918, oil on canvas, 21½ x 18" Mrs. Barnett Malbin (The Lydia and Harry Lewis Winston Collection), Birmingham, Michigan

7 *Red Carnations* c. 1919, oil on canvas, 22 x 18⅜" Mr. and Mrs. S. J. Levin, Miami Beach

8 *Flowers and Fruit* c. 1919, oil on canvas, 25 x 21" Mr. and Mrs. Henry David Epstein, New York

9 *Landscape with Figure* c. 1919, oil on canvas, 18 x 21¼" Perls Galleries, New York

10 *Reclining Woman* c. 1919, oil on canvas, 23¼ x 36½" Private collection, New York

11 *Landscape* c. 1919, oil on canvas, 18 x 24" E. and A. Silberman Galleries, New York

12 *View of Céret* c. 1919-20, oil on canvas, 21¼ x 28¾" Nathan Cummings, Chicago

13 *Landscape at Céret* c. 1920, oil on canvas, 31⅝ x 24" Galerie Beyeler, Basel, Switzerland

14 *Landscape at Céret* c. 1920-21, oil on canvas, 24 x 32" Dr. and Mrs. Howard D. Sirak, Columbus, Ohio

15 *Landscape at Céret* c. 1920-21, oil on canvas, 22 x 33" The Trustees of the Tate Gallery, London

16 *Hill at Céret* c. 1921, oil on canvas, 29¼ x 21⅝" Perls Galleries, New York

17 *View of Céret* c. 1921, oil on canvas, 29⅛ x 29½" The Baltimore Museum of Art
   Presented in Memory of George Siemonn by his Wife, Mabel Garrison Siemonn

18 *Red Roofs, Céret* c. 1921-22, oil on canvas, 32 x 25½" Henry Pearlman Foundation, New York

19 *Hill at Céret* c. 1921-22, oil on canvas, 28⅝ x 35¾" Perls Galleries, New York

20 *Landscape at Céret* c. 1922, oil on canvas, 31⅜ x 34⅛" Dr. and Mrs. Paul Todd Makler, Philadelphia

21 *Square at Céret* c. 1922, oil on canvas, 23¾ x 28¾" Dr. and Mrs. Norman F. Laskey, Mt. Kisco, New York

22 *Landscape* c. 1922-23, oil on canvas, 25¼ x 15" Mrs. Cecil Blaffer Hudson, Houston

23 *Landscape with Cypresses* c. 1922-23, oil on canvas, 25¼ x 33" Mr. and Mrs. Caleb M. Steinberg, Denver

24 *The Student* c. 1921, oil on canvas, 28⅝ x 23¾" Mrs. Evelyn Sharp, New York

25 *Praying Man* c. 1921, oil on canvas, 35⅗ x 21¼" Dr. and Mrs. Paul Todd Makler, Philadelphia

26 *Praying Man* c. 1921, oil on canvas, 50¼ x 25" Private collection, Los Angeles

27 *Portrait of a Woman* c. 1922, oil on canvas, 45¾ x 22⅞" Mr. and Mrs. Gregor Piatigorsky, Los Angeles

28 *Little Pastry Cook* c. 1922, oil on canvas, 60¼ x 26" Portland Art Museum

29 *Landscape with Flight of Stairs* c. 1922-23, oil on canvas, 32 x 25" Mrs. Margaret Sangster, Cheshire, England

30 *The Old Mill* c. 1922-1923, oil on canvas, 26⅛ x 32⅜" The Museum of Modern Art, New York
Vladimir Horowitz and Bernard Davis Funds

31 *Landscape at Cagnes* c. 1923-24, oil on canvas, 25½ x 31¾" Dr. and Mrs. Howard D. Sirak, Columbus, Ohio

32 *Landscape at Cagnes* c. 1923-24, oil on canvas, 21½ x 25¾" Mrs. Sybil H. Perry, New Haven, Connecticut

33 *Farm Girl* c. 1922-23, oil on canvas, 31½ x 17½" Dr. and Mrs. Harry Bakwin, New York

34 *Self Portrait* c. 1922-23, oil on canvas, 31⅞ x 24¾" Musée d'Art Moderne de la Ville de Paris

35 *Pastry Cook* c. 1923, oil on canvas, 25½ x 19" Joseph H. Hazen, New York

36 *Boy in Blue* c. 1924, oil on canvas, 36½ x 29" Mr. and Mrs. Henry F. Fischbach, New York

37 *Portrait of a Man* c. 1924, oil on canvas, 36 x 28" Mr. and Mrs. Gregor Piatigorsky, Los Angeles

38 *Woman on Blue Ground* c. 1924-25, oil on canvas, 24⅜ x 19¾" Musée d'Art Moderne de La Ville de Paris

39 *Woman in Pink* c. 1924-25, oil on canvas, 28½ x 21¼" Mr. and Mrs. S. J. Levin, Miami Beach

40 *Woman Knitting* c. 1924-25, oil on canvas, 25½ x 32" J. Spreiregen, London

41 *Woman in Red* c. 1924-25, oil on canvas, 25 x 21" Dr. and Mrs. Harry Bakwin, New York

42 *Portrait of a Woman* c. 1924-25, oil on canvas, 32 x 22" Mr. and Mrs. Donald S. Stralem, New York

43 *Woman in Blue Dress* c. 1924-25, oil on canvas, 31⅞ x 23⅝" Musée d'Art Moderne de la Ville de Paris

44 *Girl in Pink* c. 1924-25, oil on canvas, 29 x 21½" Miss Carol Campbell Owen, Houston

45 *Girl in Pink* c. 1924-25, oil on canvas, 34½ x 25" Joseph H. Hazen, New York

46 *The Communicant* c. 1924-25, oil on canvas, 32 x 18¾" Edward G. Robinson, Beverly Hills

47 *Woman with Green Necklace* c. 1926, oil on canvas, 35½ x 31¾" Mr. and Mrs. Sydney R. Barlow, Beverly Hills

48 *Portrait of Udo Einsild* c. 1926, oil on canvas, 34½ x 20⅝" Mr. and Mrs. Herman Elkon, New York

49 *Pastry Cook* c. 1927, oil on canvas, 30⅛ x 27¼" Mr. and Mrs. Sidney F. Brody, Los Angeles

50 *Choirboy* c. 1927, oil on canvas, 24½ x 18" Mr. and Mrs. Michael Bennahum, New York

51 *Hotel Boy* c. 1927-28, oil on canvas, 28¼ x 36¾" Mr. and Mrs. Lew R. Wasserman, Beverly Hills

52 *Valet* c. 1927-28, oil on canvas, 25 x 19½" Nathan Cummings, Chicago

53 *Portrait of Madeleine Castaing* c. 1928, oil on canvas, 39⅜ x 28⅞" Metropolitan Museum of Art, New York
Bequest of Miss Adelaide Milton de Groot (1876-1967)

54 *Portrait of Maria Lani* c. 1929, oil on canvas, 28⅞ x 23½" The Museum of Modern Art, New York
Mrs. Sam A. Lewisohn Bequest

55 *Young Woman in Red* c. 1930, oil on canvas, 31⅝ x 23½" Mrs. Evelyn Sharp, New York

56 *Still Life with Red Meat* c. 1923-24, oil on canvas, 21¼ x 25⅝″ Pierre Lévy, Troyes, France

57 *Calf and Red Curtain* c. 1924, oil on canvas, 32 x 19″ Lee Vandervelde, Los Angeles

58 *Fowl on Table* c. 1924, oil on canvas, 25⅝ x 31⅞″ Dr. Lucien Kléman, Paris

59 *Still Life* c. 1924, oil on canvas, 24 x 29½″ M. Knoedler and Co., Inc., New York

60 *Still Life with Turkey* c. 1924, oil on canvas, 21¼ x 31⅞″ Pierre Lévy, Troyes, France

61 *Still Life with Fish, Eggs and Lemons* c. 1924, oil on canvas, 25½ x 31⅞″ Marlborough-Gerson Gallery, Inc., New York

62 *Still Life with Rayfish* c. 1924, oil on canvas, 32 x 25⅝″ The Cleveland Museum of Art. Gift of Hanna Fund

63 *Still Life with Rayfish* c. 1924, oil on canvas, 36 x 32″ Dr. and Mrs. Paul Todd Makler, Philadelphia

64 *Still Life with Rayfish* c. 1924, oil on canvas, 32 x 39½″ Mrs. Oscar Miestchaninoff, New York

65 *Carcass of Beef* c. 1925, oil on canvas, 45 x 31″ The Minneapolis Institute of Arts

66 *Beef* c. 1925, oil on canvas, 65⅜ x 45¼″ Stedelijk Museum, Amsterdam

67 *Rabbit* c. 1925-26, oil on canvas, 28½ x 18⅞″ Perls Galleries, New York

68 *Pheasant* c. 1925-26, oil on canvas, 10⅝ x 39⅜″ Dr. Lucien Kléman, Paris

69 *Pheasants* c. 1926, oil on canvas, 21⅝ x 14⅛″ Galerie André Urban, Paris

70 *Fowl* c. 1926, oil on canvas, 38 x 28½″ Private collection, New York

71 *Hanging Turkey* c. 1926, oil on canvas, 36 x 28½″ Richard S. Zeisler, New York

72 *Small Town Square, Vence* c. 1930, oil on canvas, 28 x 18¼″ Art Institute of Chicago. Joseph Winterbotham Collection

73 *Tree at Vence* c. 1930, oil on canvas, 32 x 24¼″ Mrs. Lloyd Bruce Wescott, Rosemont, New Jersey

74 *Waiting Maid* c. 1933, oil on canvas, 18⅜ x 16⅛″ Mrs. Andrew Best, London

75 *Servant Girl in Blue* c. 1934, oil on canvas, 20¼ x 20⅝″ The Ritter Foundation, New York

76 *Small Boy* c. 1934, oil on canvas, 20¼ x 14¾″ Comdr. Sir Michael Culme-Seymour, Bt., Leicestershire, England

77 *Sleeping Woman* c. 1934, oil on canvas, 16 x 13″ Mrs. and Mrs. John A. Beck, Houston

78 *Portrait of a Young Woman* c. 1935, oil on canvas, 20 x 18″ Mrs. H. Harris Jonas, New York

79 *Portrait of a Man* c. 1935, oil on canvas, 22 x 13¼″ Dr. and Mrs. Harry Bakwin, New York

80 *French Cook* c. 1936, oil on panel, 26 x 18″ Mr. and Mrs. Rodney L. White, New York

81 *Woman in Profile* c. 1937, oil on canvas, 18½ x 11″ The Phillips Collection, Washington, D.C.

82 *The Old House* c. 1934, oil on canvas, 18¼ x 24¼″ Mr. and Mrs. David Finkle, New York

83 *Landscape* c. 1936, oil on canvas, 23¼ x 28¼″ Perls Galleries, New York

84 *The Tree* c. 1937, oil on canvas, 28 x 25″ Alfred Hitchcock, Los Angeles

85 *Windy Day, Auxerre* c. 1939, oil on canvas, 19½ x 25⅝″ The Phillips Collection, Washington, D.C.

86 *Trees at Auxerre* c. 1939, oil on canvas, 28¾ x 23¼″ Mr. and Mrs. Otto Edler, London

87 *Return from School after the Storm* c. 1939, oil on canvas, 17 x 19½″ The Phillips Collection, Washington, D.C.

88 *Two Children on a Road* c. 1939, oil on canvas, 15⅝ x 12½″ Perls Galleries, New York

89 *Girl at Fence* c. 1942, oil on canvas, 33 x 25½″ Nathan Cummings, Chicago

90 *Woman with Umbrella* c. 1942, oil on canvas, 20⅞ x 13¾″ Edmond Safra, Geneva

2 *Still Life with Lemons*   c. 1916, oil on canvas, 25¾ x 21½″   Mr. and Mrs. Irving Levick

4 *Spotted Vase*   c. 1917, oil on canvas, 25⅝ x 18″   Andras Kalman

6 *Red Gladioli* c. 1918, oil on canvas, 21½ x 18″ Mrs. Barnett Malbin (The Lydia and Harry Lewis Winston Collection)

8 *Flowers and Fruit* c. 1919, oil on canvas, 25 x 21″ Mr. and Mrs. Henry David Epstein

11 *Landscape* c. 1919, oil on canvas, 18 x 24″   E. and A. Silberman Galleries

9 *Landscape with Figure* c. 1919, oil on canvas, 18 x 21¼″ Perls Galleries

16 *Hill at Céret* c. 1921, oil on canvas, 29¼ x 21⅝″ Perls Galler

13 *Landscape at Céret*   c. 1920, oil on canvas, 31⅝ x 24″   Galerie Beyeler, Basel, Switzerland

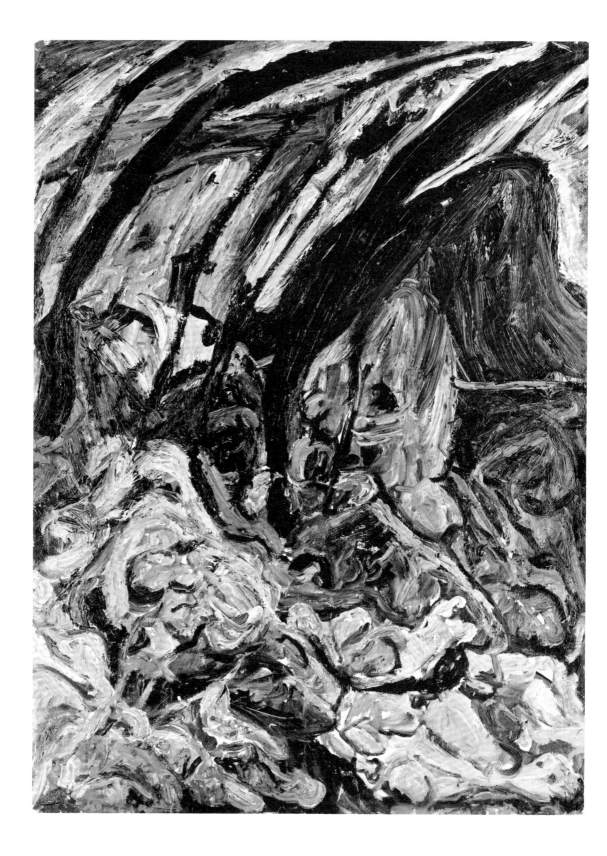

15 *Landscape at Céret* c. 1920-21, oil on canvas, 22 x 33"   The Trustees of the Tate Gallery

14 *Landscape at Céret*   c. 1920-21, oil on canvas, 24 x 32″   Dr. and Mrs. Howard D. Sirak

18 *Red Roofs, Céret* c. 1921-22, oil on canvas, 32 x 25½″ Henry Pearlman Foundation

20 *Landscape at Céret* c. 1922, oil on canvas, 31⅜ x 34⅛″ Dr. and Mrs. Paul Todd Makler

22 *Landscape* c. 1922-23, oil on canvas, 25¼ x 15″ Mrs. Cecil Blaffer Hudson.

23 *Landscape with Cypresses*   c. 1922-23, oil on canvas, 25¼ x 33″   Mr. and Mrs. Caleb M. Steinberg

27 *Portrait of a Woman* c. 1922, oil on canvas, 45¾ x 22⅞″ Mr. and Mrs. Gregor Piatigorsky

24 *The Student* c. 1921, oil on canvas, 28⅝ x 23¾″ Mrs. Evelyn Sharp

29 *Landscape with Flight of Stairs* c. 1922-23, oil on canvas, 32 x 25″ Mrs. Margaret Sangster

Praying Man c. 1921, oil on canvas, 50¼ x 25″ Private collection

30 *The Old Mill* c. 1922-1923, oil on canvas, 26⅛ x 32⅜″   The Museum of Modern Art, Vladimir Horowitz and Bernard Davis Funds

32 *Landscape at Cagnes* c. 1923-24, oil on canvas, 21½ x 25¾″ Mrs. Sybil H. Perry

34 *Self Portrait* c. 1922-23, oil on canvas, 31⅞ x 24¾″ Musée d'Art Moderne de la Ville de Pa

33 *Farm Girl*   c. 1922-23, oil on canvas, 31½ x 17½″   Dr. and Mrs. Harry Bakwin

35 *Pastry Cook* c. 1923, oil on canvas, 25½ x 19″ Joseph H. Hazen

37 *Portrait of a Man* c. 1924, oil on canvas, 36 x 28″ Mr. and Mrs. Gregor Piatigorsky

39 *Woman in Pink* c. 1924-25, oil on canvas, 28½ x 21¼″ Mr. and Mrs. S. J. Le

41 *Woman in Red* c. 1924-25, oil on canvas, 25 x 21″ Dr. and Mrs. Harry Bakwin

43 *Woman in Blue Dress*   c. 1924-25, oil on canvas, 31⅞ x 23⅝″   Musée d'Art Moderne de la Ville de Paris

44 *Girl in Pink* c. 1924-25, oil on canvas, 29 x 21½″ Miss Carol Campbell Owen

47 *Woman with Green Necklace* c. 1926, oil on canvas, 35½ x 31¾″ Mr. and Mrs. Sydney R. Barlow

46 *The Communicant*   c. 1924-25, oil on canvas, 32 x 18¾″   Edward G. Robinson

48 *Portrait of Udo Einsild*   c. 1926, oil on canvas, 34½ x 20⅝″   Mr. and Mrs. Herman Elkon

51 *Hotel Boy* c. 1927-28, oil on canvas, 28¼ x 36¾" Mr. and Mrs. Lew R. Wasserman

52 *Valet*   c. 1927-28, oil on canvas, 25 x 19½″   Nathan Cummings

53 *Portrait of Madeleine Castaing* c. 1928, oil on canvas, 39⅜ x 28⅞″ Metropolitan Museum, Miss Adelaide Milton de Groot Bequest

54 *Portrait of Maria Lani* c. 1929, oil on canvas, 28⅞ x 23½″ The Museum of Modern Art, Mrs. Sam A. Lewisohn Bequest

56 *Still Life with Red Meat* c. 1923-24, oil on canvas, 21¼ x 25⅝″ Pierre Lévy

58 *Fowl on Table* c. 1924, oil on canvas, 25⅝ x 31⅞″ Dr. Lucien Kléman

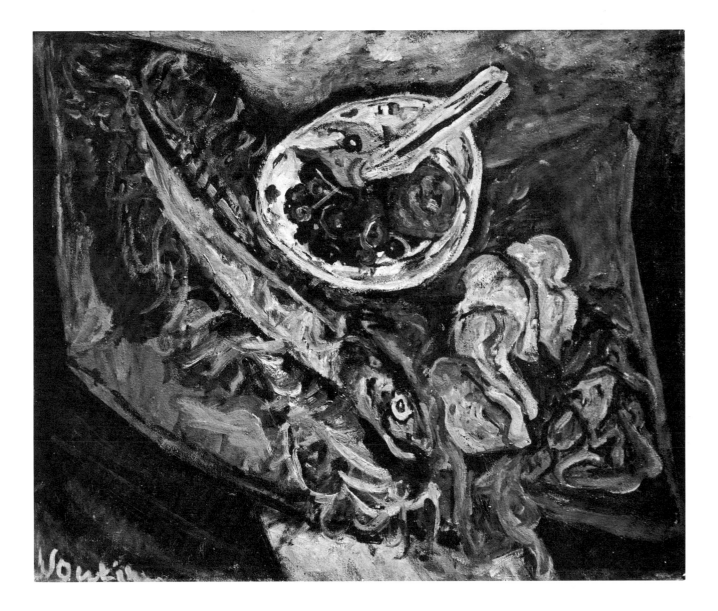

60 *Still Life with Turkey*   c. 1924, oil on canvas, 21¼ x 37⅞″   Pierre Lévy

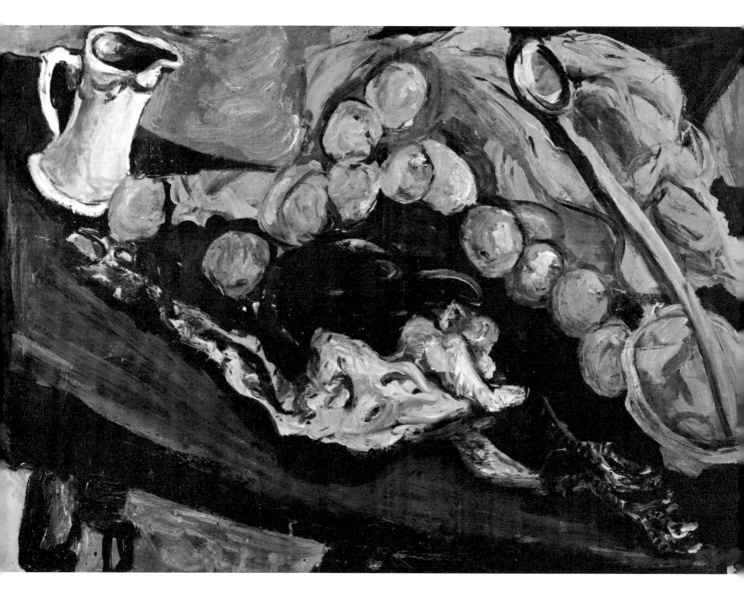

62 *Still Life with Rayfish*   c. 1924, oil on canvas, 32 x 25⅝"   The Cleveland Museum of Art. Gift of Hanna Fund

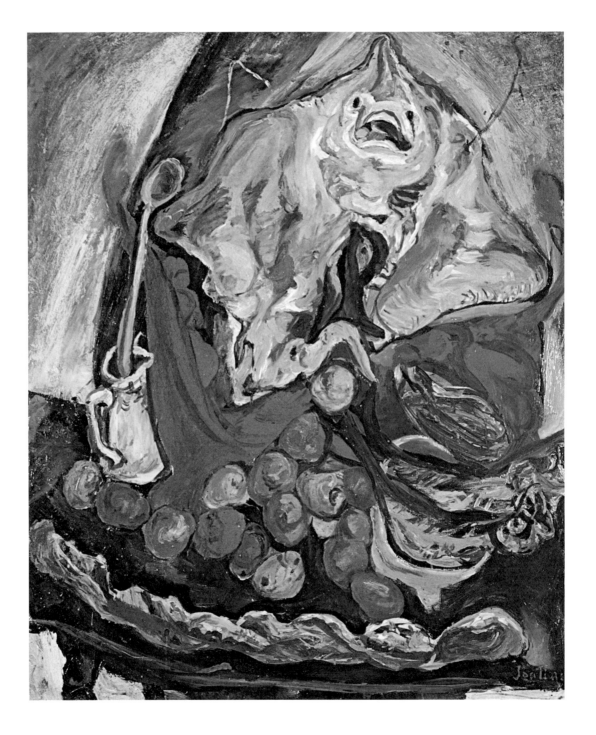

64 *Still Life with Rayfish* c. 1924, oil on canvas, 32 x 39½"   Mrs. Oscar Miestchaninoff

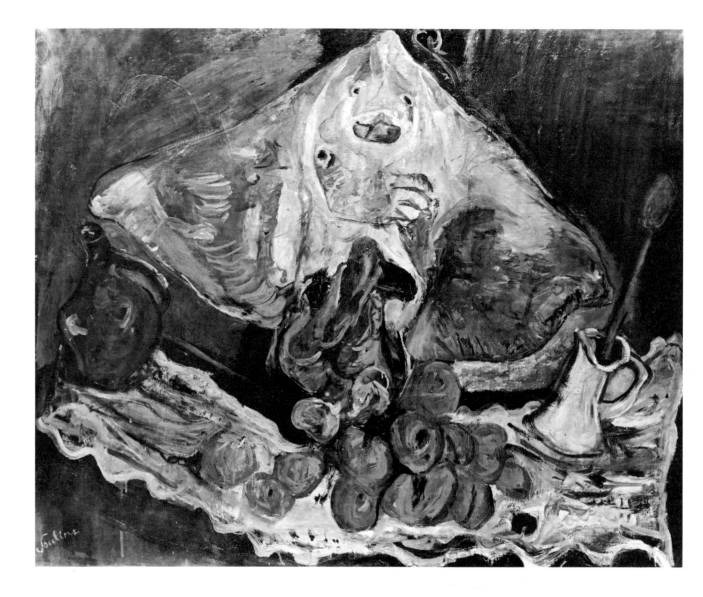

Beef   c. 1925, oil on canvas, 65⅜ x 45¼″   Stedelijk Museum

68 *Pheasant* c. 1925-26, oil on canvas, 10⅝ x 39⅜″ Dr. Lucien Kléman

70 *Fowl* c. 1926, oil on canvas, 38 x 28½″ Private collection

74 *Waiting Maid* c. 1933, oil on canvas, 18⅜ x 16⅛″ Mrs. Andrew Best

76 *Small Boy* c. 1934, oil on canvas, 20¼ x 14¾″ Comdr. Sir Michael Culme-Seymour, Bt.

77 *Sleeping Woman* c. 1934, oil on canvas, 16 x 13″ Mrs. and Mrs. John A. Beck

80 *French Cook* c. 1936, oil on panel, 26 x 18″ Mr. and Mrs. Rodney L. Wh

79 *Portrait of a Man*   c. 1935, oil on canvas, 22 x 13¼″   Dr. and Mrs. Harry Bakwin

85 *Windy Day, Auxerre* c. 1939, oil on canvas, 19½ x 25⅝″ The Phillips Collection

83 *Landscape* c. 1936, oil on canvas, 23¼ x 28¼″   Perls Galleries

88 *Two Children on a Road* c. 1939, oil on canvas, 15⅝ x 12½″ Perls Galleries

I have no recollection of my first encounter with Soutine's work. I must have known about Soutine by the early thirties. I recall an exhibition of French moderns in the Museum of Modern Art where I saw for the first time Soutine's "Beef." I thought then (I don't recall the year) that it was the best and most powerful painting in the exhibition. It made everything else look too decorative.

In the thirties Soutine was popular with and influenced a number of social realist painters — among them Jack Levine. The advanced painters that I met on the WPA project leaned mostly towards Cubism, Constructivism and Surrealism. Mondrian was beginning to be a great influence.

In the late forties the rise of abstract expressionism with some roots in surrealism and in Freud was a rebellion against Cubism, Constructivism, geometric painting and social realism — the European schools. The trend towards abstraction removed it too far from Soutine whose work was grounded in direct observation of nature. The Abstract Expressionists' belief in spontaneity and in an actively articulated surface disposed the painters of that movement towards an appreciation of Soutine. But Soutine, essentially tradition based, was crowded out of modern art history by anti-traditionalist art movements. So that no matter how big his personal stature was, his influence on other painters was not too significant. I personally know of no abstract expressionist painters whose work showed a Soutine influence. The exception may be De Kooning whose interest in Soutine may have had some influence on his "Woman" series — but this is a speculation that I cannot base on anything factual.

I myself was intensely moved by Soutine and still am. But my commitment towards abstraction, the trend away from working from nature, left little room for a Soutine influence.

On the whole, my judgment is that Abstract Expressionism influenced a deeper appreciation of Soutine but that his influence was sidestepped by the urge towards abstraction.

Jack Tworkov

BOOKS AND ARTICLES
Chronological

1923   1   Guillaume, Paul. "Soutine," *Arts à Paris* (Paris), no. 7, January, pp. 5-6.

1924   2   Barnes, Albert C. "Soutine," *Arts à Paris* (Paris), no. 10, November, pp. 6-8.

1925   3   Barnes, Albert C. *The Art in Painting,* New York, Harcourt, Brace, pp. 115, 283, 305, 307, 326-330, 3 illus.

1926   4   George, Waldemar. "Soutine," *Amour de l'Art* (Paris), vol. 7, no. 11, Nov., pp. 367-370, illus.

1928   5   George, Waldemar. *Artistes Juifs: Soutine,* Paris Editions "Le Triangle." 16 pages of text, 16 plates.

1929   6   Faure, Elie. *Soutine,* Paris, Editions Crès. 12 pages of text, 32 illus. [Reprinted 1934 with additions: *Ombres solides,* Paris, Société française d'éditions litteraires et techniques.]

1930   7   Drieu la Rochelle, Pierre. "Soutine," *Formes* (Paris), no. 5, May, pp. 4-5.

1932   8   Sachs, Maurice. "Soutine," *Creative Art,* vol. 11, no. 4, December, pp. 272-278.

1933   9   George, Waldemar. "Soutine et la violence dramatique," *Amour de l'Art* (Paris), vol. 14, pp. 150-152. [Reprinted in René Huyghe, *Histoire de l'art Contemporain, la peinture,* Paris, Alcan, 1935, pp. 150-152 et passim. Biographic and bibliographic notes p. 152.]

1942   10   Georges — Michel, Michel. *Peintres et sculpteurs j'ai connus, 1900-1942,* New York, Brentano's, pp. 180-190.

1943   11   Sachs, Maurice. "Contres les peintures d'aujourd'hui," *La Nouvelle Revue Française* (Paris), vol. 43, July, pp. 28-42; Soutine, pp. 39-40.

1944   12   Collié, Andrée. "Souvenirs sur Soutine," *Le Spectateur des Arts,* (Paris), no. 1, December, pp. 14-18.

      13   Serouya, Henri. "Soutine," *Les Lettres Françaises* (Paris), December 2.

1945   14   Cogniat, Raymond. *Soutine,* Paris, Editions du Chêne. 11 pages of text, 45 plates.

1950   15   Tworkov, Jack. "The Wandering Soutine," *Art News,* vol. 47, no. 7, part I, November, pp. 30-33, 62, illus. pp. 30-33.

1951   16   Hess, Thomas B. *Abstract Painting,* New York, Viking, pp. 69-70, ill.

      17   Lipchitz, Jacques and Dorothy Gees Seckler. "I Remember Modigliani," *Art News,* vol. 49, no. 10, February, pp. 26-29, 64-65.

      18   Orloff, Chana. "Mon ami Soutine," *Preuves* (Paris), November, pp. 17-21. [Reprinted in abridged English translation, *Jewish Chronicle* (London), November 1, 1963.]

1952   19   Cogniat, Raymond. *Soutine,* Geneva, Paris, New York, Skira. 2 pages of text; biographical and bibliographical information; 6 plates.

      20   Werner, Alfred. "Chaim Soutine: Self-Liberation Through Art," *Chicago Jewish Forum,* vol. 10, no. 3, Spring, pp. 176-184, illus. pp. 177, 179, 181.

1953   21   Greenberg, Clement. "Books in Review: Two of the Moderns," *Commentary,* vol. 16, no. 4, October, pp. 386-389. [Review of bibl. 19.]

1954   22   Lassaigne, Jacques. *Soutine,* Paris, Hazan. 7 pages of text, 20 plates.

1955   23   Szittya, Emile. *Soutine et son temps,* Paris, La Bibliothèque des Arts. 125 pages including 19 illustrations, chronology and bibliography.

1956   24   Fels, Florent. "Haim Soutine," *L'Art Vivant de 1900 à nos jours: 1914-1950,* vol. II, Geneva, Cailler.

      25   "Garde, Mlle." (Gerda Groth). "Mes années chez Soutine (propos recueilles par M. Ragon)," *L'Oeil* (Paris), January. [Reprinted in English translation, *The Selective Eye,* Lausanne, Bernier; New York, Reynal, 1956/1957, pp. 142-146.]

1957   26   D'Ancona, Paolo. *Some Aspects of Expressionism: Modigliani, Chagall, Soutine, Pascin,* Milan, Edizioni del Milione, pp. 51-67, 9 plates.

1959   27   George, Waldemar. *Soutine,* Paris, Art et Style. 7 pages of text, 31 plates.

1960   28   Courthion, Pierre. *Soutine.* [Unpublished manuscript translated into English by Mrs. Eleanor Levieux.]

      29   Serouya, Henri. *Soutine.* [Unpublished manuscript in French.]

1961   30   Greenberg, Clement. *Art and Culture,* Boston, Beacon Press, pp. 115-119.

      31   Sperber, Manes. "Sur l'art juif," *L'Arche* (Paris), August-September.

1963   32   Castaing, Marcellin and Jean Leymarie. *Soutine,* Paris and Lausanne, La Bibliothèque des Arts. 33 pages of text; 45 plates. [English translation, New York, Abrams, 1963.]

      33   Sylvester, David. "Soutine," *The Sunday Times Colour Magazine* (London), September 15, pp. 3-9, illus. pp. 3-9.

1964   34   Tuchman, Maurice. "Portraits de Soutine," *Art de France* (Paris), vol. IV, pp. 206-217, illus. pp. 207-217.

1966   35   Forge, Andrew. *Soutine,* London, Spring Books. 38 pages of text and illustrations; 48 plates. [Selection of paintings drawn from Arts Council of Great Britain catalog; see bibl. 119.]

      36   Gimpel, René. *Diary of an Art Dealer,* New York, Farrar, Strauss and Giroux, pp. 362, 365, 372, 376, 377, 378-379, 381.

      37   Negri, Renata. *Soutine,* Milan, Fratelli Fabri. 5 pages of text and illustrations; 15 color plates.

EXHIBITIONS, CATALOGS, REVIEWS

Chronological

1927   Paris, Galerie Bing.

38 Review: Charensol, Georges. "Soutine."
Art Vivant (Paris), vol. 3, 1927, p. 547.

1930   Paris, Théatre Pigalle. May. [Group exhibition
sponsored by *Art Vivant*.] 4 works.

39 Review: Gauthier, Maxmilien. "Notices
Bio-bibliographiques: Soutine," *Art Vivant* (Paris),
vol. 6, no. 30, May 15, 1930, pp. 417, 431, ill. p. 422.

1935 40 Chicago, Arts Club. December. 20 works.
Catalog with text by Edouard-Joseph, translated
from bibl. 140.

1936 41 New York, Valentine Gallery. February.
21 works. Catalog.

42 Reviews: Sayre, Ann Hamilton. "Soutine of
the Ecole de Paris in His First New York
Exhibit," *Art News*, vol. 34, no. 19, February 8,
1936, pp. 5, 7, illus. p. 7.

43 "Tortured Forms," *Art Digest*, vol. 10, no. 10,
February 15, 1936, p. 12.

1936   New York, Mrs. Cornelius J. Sullivan Gallery.
February-March. 14 works.

44 Review: Sayre, Ann Hamilton. "New Exhibitions of the Week: The Early and Mature Work
of Chaim Soutine," *Art News*, vol. 34, no. 23,
March 7, 1936, p. 10.

1937   New York, Mrs. Cornelius J. Sullivan Gallery.
March-April. 15 works.

45 Reviews: Breuning, Margaret. "Current Exhibitions:
Notes," *Parnassus*, vol. 9, no. 4, April 1937, p. 44.

46 D[avidson], M[artha]. "New Exhibitions of the
Week: The Growth of Soutine's Magnificent
Talent," *Art News*, vol. 35, no. 28, April 10,
1937, pp. 14-15.

1937 47 London, The Leicester Galleries. April.
33 Works. Catalog with text by Maurice Sachs,
reprinted from bibl. 6.

48 Review: *Apollo*, vol. 25, May 1937, p. 297.
New York, Valentine Gallery. May.

49 Reviews: Bird, Paul. "A Soutine Boom?," *Art
Digest*, vol. 11, no. 16, May 15, 1937, p. 20, ill. p. 20.

50 Breuning, Margaret. "Seeing the Shows:
Soutine," *Magazine of Art*, vol. 30, no. 6,
June 1937, pp. 388-389.

51 D[avidson], M[artha]. "New Exhibitions of
the Week: Soutine in His Most Important
American Show," *Art News*, vol. 35, no. 32,
May 8, 1937, p. 15, ill. p. 15.

52 "'Eliptic Emotions,'" *Art Digest*, vol. 11, no. 17,
June 1937, p. 22.

1937 53 Paris, Petit Palais, "Les Maîtres de l'art
Independant, 1895-1937." June-October.
12 works. Catalog with text by Albert Sarraut.

1938   London, Storran Gallery. November. 12 works.

1939   New York, Valentine Gallery. March-April.
23 works.

54 Reviews: Brian, Doris. "Soutine Turns to
Classicism: His Recent and Earlier Manner
Contrasted in a New Show," *Art News*, vol. 37,
no. 25, March 18, 1939, p. 7, illus. p. 7.

55 "Some Call it Classic," *Art Digest*, vol. 13,
no. 13, April 1, 1939, p. 17, ill. p. 17.

56 Sweeney, James Johnson. "Exhibitions in
New York: Twenty-three Paintings by Soutine,"
Parnassus, vol. 11, no. 4, April 1939, pp. 21-22.

57 "Van Gogh of Our Time," *Newsweek*, March 27,
1939, p. 27.

1940 58 New York, Carroll Carstairs Gallery.
April-May. 12 works. Catalog with text by
Henry McBride.

59 Reviews: Lowe, Jeannett. "The New and the
Old Soutine: Cross-Section of the Emotional
Painter," *Art News*, vol. 38, no. 29, April 20,
1940, pp. 11, 21, illus. p. 11.

60 "New York Sees Soutine, Tragic Lithuanian," *Art
Digest*, vol. 14, no. 14, April 15, 1940, p. 9, ill. p. 9.

61 McCausland, Elizabeth. "Exhibitions in New
York: Three Frenchmen: Rouault, Soutine,
Derain," *Parnassus*, vol. 12, no. 5, May 1940, p. 40.

1943 62 Washington, D.C., Phillips Memorial Gallery.
January-February. 23 works. Catalog with
text by Duncan Phillips.

1943 63 New York, Bignou Gallery, March-April.
18 works. Catalog with text by Albert C. Barnes.

64 Reviews: "The Passing Shows: Chaim Soutine,"
Art News, vol. 42, no. 4, Apr. 1, 1943, p. 23, ill. p. 23.

65 R[iley], M[aude]. "Placing Soutine," *Art Digest*,
vol. 17, no. 13, April 1, 1943, p. 17, ill. p. 17.

1944 66 New York, Niveau Gallery. October. 13 works.
Catalog with text by Michel Georges-Michel.

67 Reviews: Breuning, Margaret. "Soutine
Memorial," *Art Digest*, vol. 19, no. 2,
October 15, 1944, p. 15.

68 F[rost], R[osamund]. "In Memoriam: Soutine
Over 20 Years," *Art News*, vol. 43, no. 13,
October 15, 1944, p. 14, ill. p. 14.

1944   Paris, Salon d'Automne. [For comment, see bibl. 12.]

1945 69 Paris, Galerie de France, "Retrospective
Soutine, 1894-1943." January. 40 works.
Catalog with text by Louis Parrot.

70 Review: *Arts* (Paris), no. 1, January 31, 1945, p. 1.

71 Boston, Institute of Modern Art, "Chagall and Soutine." January-February. 23 works. Catalog: *Art Panorama, An Illustrated Catalog,* Boston, 1945, pp. 13-16, ill. p. 15.

1947 72 London, Gimpel fils, "Soutine: 1895-1943." April-May. 18 works. Catalog with text by Maurice Collis.

1947　Paris, Galerie Zak. Nov.-Dec. 19 works.

73 Reviews: *Arts* (Paris), no. 143, Dec. 5, 1947, p. 2.

74 Boers, Frans. "Kroniek: Soutine." *Kroniek van Kunst en Kultuur* (Amsterdam), vol. 9, no. 2, February 1948, p. 64.

75 Z[ahar], M[arcel]. "Soutine," *Panorama des Arts, 1947,* Paris, Aimery Somogy, 1948, pp. 239-241, ill. p. 240.

1949 76 New York, Van-Diemen-Lilienfeld Galleries, "Soutine and Utrillo." January. 7 works. Catalog.

77 Review: S[harp], M[arynell]. "Soutine and Utrillo," *Art Digest,* vol. 23, no. 8, Jan. 15, 1949, p. 14, ill. p. 14.

1950　Paris, Galerie Bernier, "Présence dans la Nature." (With Loutreuil, Marquet, Vuillard, Desnoyer and Gruber.)

1950- 78 New York, Museum of Modern Art and
1951　Cleveland Museum of Art. November 1950-March 1951. 75 works. Book-catalog with text by Monroe Wheeler; 116 pages including 77 illustrations; chronology by Jean-Pierre Brasseur; bibliography by Hanna B. Muller.

79 Reviews: Adlow, Dorothy. "Two New Shows," *Christian Science Monitor Magazine,* November 11, 1959, p. 8, ill. p. 8.

80 "Art: Hot and Heavy," *Time,* vol. 56, no. 20, November 13, 1950, p. 44, illus. p. 44.

81 Breuning, Margaret. "The Cataclysmic World of Chaim Soutine," *Art Digest,* vol. 25, no. 4, November 15, 1950, p. 11, illus. p. 11.

82 Burrows, Carlyle. "Soutine on Exhibit at Museum of Modern Art," *New York Herald Tribune,* November 1, 1950.

83 Francis, Henry S. "Important Exhibitions, January and February, 1951," *The Bulletin of the Cleveland Museum of Art,* vol. 38, no. 1,

84 Greenberg, Clement. "Art Chronicle: Chaim Soutine," *Partisan Review,* vol. 18, no. 1, January-February 1951, pp. 82-87.

85 H[ess], T[homas] B. "The Coming Season: Pioneers of the Avant-Garde," *Art News,* vol. 49, no. 6, Oct. 1950, pp. 13, 57, ill. p. 13.

1951 86 London, Royal Academy of Arts, "L'Ecole de Paris." 4 works. Catalog with text by Jean Cassou.

1951　San Francisco, California Palace of the Legion of Honor, "Miró and Soutine." December.

87 Review: Ballard, Louise. "Art," *Arts and Architecture,* vol. 68, no. 11, Dec. 1951, p. 11.

1952 88 Venice, XXVI Venice Biennal Exhibition. 35 works. Catalog with text by Jean Leymarie, pp. 178-183.

89 Reviews: Arcangeli, Francesco. "Corot e Soutine a Venezia," *Paragone,* no. 33, 1952, pp. 58-64.

90 Guzzi, Virgilio. "The XXVIth Biennal Exhibition at Venice," *East and West,* vol. 3, no. 3, Oct. 1952, pp. 179-188, ill. p. 182 (Soutine p. 184).

91 Veronesi, Guilia. "Chaim Soutine," *Emporium,* vol. 116, 1952, pp. 48-52.

92 Zervos, Christian. "Coup d'oeil sur la XXVIe Biennale de Venice," *Cahiers d'Art,* vol. 27, part 2, 1952, pp. 273-287 (Soutine pp. 278, 280-281).

1953　Paris, Galerie Andre Weil. September. [Exhibition sponsored by the Société des Amis de Soutine.]

93 Review: Serullaz, Maurice. "D'une exposition à l'autre: Soutine," *France Illustration,* no. 402, September 1953, p. 68, illus. pp. 68, 69.

1953 94 London, Redfern Gallery, "Russian Emigre Artists in Paris." November. 4 works. Catalog with text by Alexander Watt.

1953 95 New York, Perls Galleries. November-December. 21 works. Catalog.

96 Reviews: Coates, Robert M. "The Art Galleries: Soutine and Modigliani," *New Yorker,* vol. 29, no. 40, Nov. 21, 1953, pp. 105-106, 108, 110.

97 G[uest], B[arbara]. "Reviews and Previews: Chaim Soutine," *Art News,* vol. 52, no. 8, December 1953, p. 42, ill. p. 42.

98 Werner, Alfred. "New York: Soutine: Affinity for an Alien World," *Art Digest,* vol. 28, no. 4, November 15, 1953, pp. 17-18, ill. p. 17.

1954 99 New York, Perls Galleries, "The William March Collection of Modern French Masters." October-November. 9 works. Catalog.

1956 100 Paris, Maison de la Pensée Française, "Soutine, 1894-1943." March-April. 26 works. Catalog with text by Elie Faure.

101 Reviews: "Painters of Rage and Storm," *Time,* vol. 67, no. 21, May 21, 1956, p. 92, ill. p. 93.

102 Schneider, Pierre. "Art News from Paris: Soutine, Barye," *Art News,* vol. 55, no. 3, May 1956, p. 16.

1956 103 Chicago, Arts Club. October. 16 works. Catalog.

104 Review: Speyer, James A. "Art News from Chicago," *Art News,* vol. 55, no. 8, December 1956, p. 49.

1958 105 New York, Hirschl and Adler Galleries, Inc., "Soutine and His Circle in Paris." June. 7 works. Catalog with text by Arbit Blatas.

106 Reviews: Hoffmann, Edith. "Current and Forthcoming Exhibitions: New York," *The Burlington Magazine,* vol. 100, no. 665, August 1958, p. 296.

107 P[orter], F[airfield]. "Reviews and Previews: Soutine and His Circle in Paris," *Art News,* vol. 57, no. 4, Summer 1958, p. 16.

1959 108 Paris, Galerie Charpentier, "Cent Tableaux de Soutine." Fall. 119 works. Catalog with text by Waldemar George and M. Castaing.

109 Reviews: Berger, René. "L'Eté à Paris," *XXe Siècle,* vol. 21, no. 13, December 1959 (supplement), p. 50, ill. p. 51.

110 Mock, Jean Yves. "Notes from Paris and London: Soutine at the Galerie Charpentier," *Apollo,* vol. 70, no. 415, September 1959, p. 60, ill. p. 60.

111 Schneider, Pierre. "Art News from Paris: Russian Expressionists." *Art News,* vol. 58, no. 6, September 1959, p. 47.

112 Sylvester, David. "Soutine Reconsidered in Paris Exhibition," *The New York Times,* September 6, 1959.

113 Watt, Alexander. "Paris Commentary," *Studio,* vol. 158, no. 799, November 1959, pp. 123-124, ill. p. 122.

1959 114 Manchester, Crane Gallery, "Soutine and His Circle." December. 1 work. Catalog.

1959 115 New York, Knoedler Gallery, "Paintings, Watercolors and Sculpture from the Collection of Mr. and Mrs. Henry Pearlman." January-February. 6 works. Catalog.

1960 116 London, Crane Kalman Gallery, "Soutine and His Circle." March-April. 4 works. Catalog.

117 Reviews: Duerden, Dennis. "Soutine and His Circle," *Art News and Review,* vol. 12, no. 7, April 27-May 3, 1960.

118 Shipp, Horace. "Current Shows and Comments: The Dark is Light Enough," *Apollo,* vol. 71, no. 422, April 1960, p. 92

1960 119 New York, Knoedler Gallery, "The Colin Collection: Paintings, Watercolors, Drawings and Sculpture." April-May. 16 works. Catalog.

1963 120 London, Tate Gallery and Edinburgh Arts Festival. August-November 1963. 57 works. Retrospective organized by the Arts Council of Great Britain, directed by David Sylvester. Catalog with essay by David Sylvester and catalog notes by Maurice Tuchman; 28 pages including 32 illustrations. [Essay reprinted in abridged form: "Soutine, The Impact of Infighting," *Art News,* vol. 62, no. 6, October 1963, pp. 22-27, 48-52, illus. pp. 22-27.]

121 Reviews: Amaya, Mario. "Modigliani — Soutine," *Financial Times* (London), October 1, 1963.

122 Baro, Gene. "International Reports: Abundance and Synthesis," *Arts,* vol. 38, no. 3, December 1963, pp. 41-42, ill. p. 41.

123 Brett, Guy. "Modigliani and Soutine at the Tate," *Manchester Guardian,* October 1, 1963.

124 Burn, Guy. "Soutine and Modigliani," *Arts Review* (London), October 5, 1963, p. 3.

125 Dickson, Elder T. "International and Scottish Painting at the Edinburgh Festival," *Studio International,* vol. 166, no. 847, November 1963, pp. 204-205, ill. p. 203.

126 Forge, Andrew. "Discovery," *New Statesman,* October 4, 1963, p. 456.

127 Hall, Douglas. "The Stature of Soutine," *Apollo,* vol. 78, no. 20 (new series), October 1963, p. 310, ill. p. 311.

128 Irwin, David. "Current and Forthcoming Exhibitions: Edinburgh," *The Burlington Magazine,* vol. 105, no. 727, October 1963, pp. 462, 465, illus, p. 464.

129 Melville, Robert. "Retrospective at the Tate," *Architectural Review,* vol. 134, November 1963, p. 360.

130 "Modigliani and Soutine — Two Painters of the 20th Century," *Illustrated London News,* September 14, 1963, p. 389, illus.

131 Russell, John. "The World of Art: Outcast among the Great," *The Sunday Times* (London), August 18.

132 Smith, Sydney Goodsir. "Works by Contrasting Masters," *The Scotsman* (Edinburgh), August 19, 1963.

133 Stone, Peter. "Pictures from an Exhibition: Modigliani and Soutine at the Tate," *Jewish Chronicle* (London), Oct. 4, 1963, p. 7, ill. p. 7.

1963 134 London, Crane Kalman Gallery, "Soutine-Modigliani et Leur Temps." October. 1 work. Catalog.

1964 135 New York, The Solomon R. Guggenheim Museum, "Van Gogh and Expressionism." July-September. 5 works. Catalog with text by Maurice Tuchman.

1966 136 Paris, Orangerie des Tuileries, "Collection Jean Walter-Paul Guillaume." 22 works. Catalog with text by Michele Bundorf and catalog notes.

137 Review: de Forges, M. T. and G. Allemand. "Orangerie des Tuileries: La Collection Jean Walter-Paul Guillaume," *Revue du Louvre,* vol. 16, no. 1, 1966, p. 64.

OTHER REFERENCES
Chronological

1927 138 Raynal, Maurice.
           *Anthologie de la peinture
           en France de 1906 à nos jours,*
           Paris, Editions Montaigne, pp. 287-290.
           [English translation, *Modern French Painters,*
           New York, Brentano's, 1928, pp. 137-152.]

1930 139 Drieu la Rochelle, Pierre. "Soutine."
           Formes (Paris), no. 5, May, pp. 4-5.

1931 140 Bazin, Germain. "Un Nouveau Fauvism:
           Aujame," *Amour de l'art* (Paris), vol. 12,
           pp. 439-440.

1934 141 Edouard-Joseph.
           *Dictionnaire biographique
           des artistes Contemporains, 1910-30,* Paris,
           Librarie Grund, pp. 310-311.

1937 142 Escholier, Raymond.
           La peinture française XXᵉ Siècle,
           Paris, Floury, pp. 136, 138.

1940 143 Wilenski, Reginald H. *Modern French
           Painters,* New York, Reynal & Hitchcock,
           pp. 80, 238, 258, 294, 301, 315, 317.

1941 144 Douglas, Charles. *Artist Quarter:
           Reminiscences of Montmartre and
           Montparnasse,* London, Faber & Faber,
           pp. 316-320 et passim.

1942 145 Wheeler, Monroe,
           20th Century Portraits,
           New York, Museum of Modern Art, pp. 16,
           89, ill. p. 89. [Exhibition catalog.]

1944 146 Carco, Francis. *L'Ami des Peintres,* Geneva,
           Editions du Milieu du Monde, pp. 46-47.

      147 "Sifriat Poalim," Worker's Book Guild.
           *Amedeo Modigliani, Jules Pascin, Chaim
           Soutine,* Tel-Aviv.
           8 pages of text in Hebrew, illus.

1945 148 Delmas, Gladys.
           "French Art During the Occupation:
           Soutine," *Magazine of Art,*
           vol. 38, no. 3, March, pp. 87-88.

      149 Georges-Michel, Michel. *Chefs — d'oeuvre
           de peintres contemporains,* New York,
           Editions de la Maison française, pp. 201, 203.

      150 San Lazzaro, G. di. "Ricorde di Soutine,"
           Tre Arti (Milan), vol. 1, no. 1, p. 8, illus. p. 8.

1947 151 Lassaigne, Jacques. *Cent chefs-d'oeuvre des
           peintres de l'Ecole de Paris,* Paris,
           Editions de la Galerie Charpentier,
           pp. 104-106, 119-121, 200-201, illus.
           Text in French and English.

      152 Raynal, Maurice. *Peintres du XXᵉ Siècle,*
           Geneva, Skira, pp. 26-27, illus.

1953 Venturi, Lionello. *Pittura Contemporanea.*
      Milan, U. Hoepli, p. 23.

1948 154 Soby, James Thrall. "Two Painters of
           Tragedy: Rouault and Soutine," in
           Contemporary Painters, New York,
           Museum of Modern Art, pp. 12-18.

1950 155 *History of Modern Painting: Matisse, Munch,
           Rouault, Fauvism, Expressionism,* Geneva,
           Skira, pp. 122-129, 145-146.

1951 156 Georges-Michel, Michel. "Chaim Soutine,"
           Biennale di Venezia, no. 4, April, pp. 7-9,
           illus. pp. 7-9.

      157 Lassaigne, Jacques. "Présence de Soutine,"
           Revue de la Pensée Française (Paris),
           vol. 10, no. 12. December,
           pp. 41-44, illus. pp. 42-43.

      158 "A Study of Soutine," *The Times Literary
           Supplement* (London), no. 2, 570, May 4,
           pp. 269-270.

1952 159 Morris, Wright. "The Violent Land, Some
           Observations on the Faulkner Country,"
           Magazine of Art, vol. 45, no. 3, March,
           pp. 99-103, ill. p. 99.

1953 160 Michonze, Gregoire. *Les Lettres Françaises*
           (Paris), July 23-26.

1954 161 Sachs, Maurice. *Tableau des moeurs de ce
           Temps,* Paris.

1956 162 Dorival, Bernard. *Les Etapes de la peinture
           française contemporaine,* vol. 3, Paris, Gallimard,
           Gallimard, pp. 187-193, 197, 199, 200-205,
           pp. 187-193, 197, 199, 200-205, 207-208.

1958 163 Heron, Patrick. *The Changing Forms of Art,*
           New York, Noonday, pp. 146-148.

1959 164 de Mazia, Violette.
           "Continuity of Traditions in Painting,"
           Art and Education, New Jersey,
           The Barnes Foundation Press, pp. 103-116.

      165 Diwo, Jean. "Soutine le dernier maudit," *Paris
           Match,* no. 539, Aug. 8, pp. 63-69, illus. pp. 63-69.

      166 Geraldy, P. "Chaim Soutine ou l'enfant
           manque," *Le Figaro* (Paris), August.

      167 Revol, J. "Soutine, Matière Suppliciée,"
           La Nouvelle Revue Française (Paris), August.

      168 Sterling, Charles. *Still-life from Antiquity
           to the Present,* New York, Universe Books,
           pp. 53, 97, 115-117, ill. p. 103.

      169 Talphir, Gabriel. "Chaim Soutine
           (1894-1943)," *Gazith, Art and Literary
           Journal* (Tel Aviv), vol. 17, no. 195-196,
           August-September, pp. 1-3.

1960 170 Chapiro, Jacques. *La Ruche,* Paris, Flammarion,
           pp. 37-44, 50, 85-88, 101, 110, 127-128, 134, 147.

PHOTOGRAPHERS	*Plate numbers*
Victor Amato	81, 87
The Baltimore Museum of Art	17
Henry Beville	85
Galerie Beyeler	13
Brenwasser	42, 59
J. E. Bulloz	38, 43
The Art Institute of Chicago	72
The Cleveland Museum of Art	62
Ed Cornachio, John Gebhart, Robert Kays	7, 26, 27, 37, 39, 47, 49, 84
George Cserna	52, 89
Thomas Feist	48
A. Godin	56, 60
Sherwin Greenberg, McGranahan and May, Inc.	2
Peter A. Juley and Son	64, 78
A. Kilbertus	34
Joseph Klima, Jr.	5
Marlborough-Gerson Gallery, Inc.	61
James O. Milmoe	23
Metropolitan Museum of Art	53
Alfred A. Monner	28
Museum of Modern Art	11, 30, 54
O. E. Nelson	75
Biagio Pinto	63
Eric Pollitzer	33, 36, 41, 50
Percy Rainford	3, 9, 16, 19, 20, 25, 55, 63, 67, 83, 88
Photo Routhier	58, 68
John D. Schiff	71
Stedelijk Museum	66
Taylor and Dull	57
John Thomson	46, 51
Galerie André Urban	69
V. Wolfhagen	44

Tom Woodward, design
Koltun Bros., lithography
Ad Compositors, typography

26,000 copies
February 1968